COLLECTIONS

TEACHER'S EDITION
Practice Book

GRADE 4

Harcourt

Orlando   Boston   Dallas   Chicago   San Diego

Visit *The Learning Site!*
www.harcourtschool.com

Contents

TOUCH A DREAM

Printed in the United States of America

ISBN 0-15-312726-0

1 2 3 4 5 6 7 8 9 10   054   2003   2002   2001   2000

REPRODUCING COPIES FOR STUDENTS

This Teacher's Edition contains full-size student pages with answers printed in non-reproducible blue ink.

It may be necessary to adjust the exposure control on your photocopy machine to a lighter setting to ensure that blue answers do not reproduce.

Name _____

▶ **Use words from the box to complete the sentences in the letter. Some words will be used twice.**

anxious	recognizing	adore	vacant	sprucing	retire

Dear Uncle Jim,

I'm glad to be back home with Mama, Papa, and Grandma, but at the same time, I miss you. I really did **(1)** _____ adore _____ living in the city and making the **(2)** _____ vacant _____ rooftop into a flower garden paradise.

Since I've been home, I've been busy **(3)** _____ sprucing _____ up my room. I did not **(4)** _____ retire _____ as a gardener, either!

There is a **(5)** _____ vacant _____ lot outside my window where I have planted all kinds of colorful flowers. I am **(6)** _____ anxious _____ to send you a picture as soon as the flowers are in full bloom.

I'm growing even faster than the flowers. **(7)** _____ Recognizing _____ me will be a challenge for you next time I visit.

I know you still must be working hard in the bakery, since you are too young to **(8)** _____ retire _____! Please send my love to Ed and Emma, whom I **(9)** _____ adore _____.

I am **(10)** _____ anxious _____ to see you all again!

Your loving niece,
Lydia Grace

TRY THIS! Write a letter to a friend or relative, telling about an interesting project you've taken part in lately. Use at least three of the Vocabulary Words in your letter.

Harcourt

Name _____

▶ **Complete the time line below by writing important story events in the boxes.** Possible responses are given.

Important Events in Lydia Grace's Life

Date	Event
August 27, 1935	Lydia Grace learns that she will live with Uncle Jim.
September 5, 1935	Lydia Grace arrives at Uncle Jim's and likes her new home.
February 12, 1936	Lydia Grace becomes friends with Ed and Emma Beech.
March 5, 1936	Lydia Grace plants seeds and plans to use a secret place.
May 27, 1936	Lydia Grace gets plants from home; Emma helps with the secret place.
July 4, 1936	The secret place is ready. Lydia Grace expects a smile from Uncle Jim.
July 11, 1936	Uncle Jim bakes a cake for Lydia Grace, Ed, and Emma. Lydia Grace is going home.

▶ **Write a brief summary of Lydia Grace's character. Think about things she says, does, and thinks.**

Possible response: Lydia Grace enjoys growing plants and wants to make

people smile. She is a hard worker who likes to learn and help out.

Harcourt

2 Touch a Dream

Name _____

▶ **Read the story. Then complete each sentence and answer each question.** Exact wording may vary.

It was a warm May morning. Tamika and James were looking sadly at the flowers they had just planted in the back of the garden behind their house. "What were we thinking when we planted them way back there?" James said. "We knew we would have to water them, and now we can't unless we carry heavy watering cans. We have two garden hoses, but neither one of them is long enough to reach those flowers." He held up the end of the garden hose he had attached to the faucet. The hose reached only about halfway to the thirsty flowers.

Then Tamika smiled. Bending down, she joined the two hoses end to end. "Two short hoses can make one long hose," she said. "Now those flowers will have a drink of water, and we won't have to carry heavy watering cans after all."

The **characters** are **(1)** _____Tamika_____ and **(2)** _____James_____.

3. Where does the story take place? _____in Tamika and James's backyard_____

4. When does the story take place? _____on a morning in May_____

5. What is the weather like? _____warm_____

Problem: Tamika and James have just finished **(6)** _____planting some_____

_____flowers_____. They want to **(7)** _____water_____

them, but they can't because **(8)** _____their garden hoses are too short_____.

Solution: Tamika **(9)** _____puts the two hoses together_____. Now the hoses

can **(10)** _____reach the flowers_____.

TRY THIS! Create a story map to show how Tamika and James will solve the problem of paint getting into their garden, when a neighbor paints his house.

Harcourt

Name _____

▶ **Read the story. Then choose the answer that best completes each sentence. Mark the letter for that answer.**

One afternoon in spring, Dawn was looking at the straight rows in Grandpa's garden. Suddenly she called, "Look! A bunny! Grandpa, it hopped right over your tomato plants!"

"Oh, no," Grandpa groaned. "That rabbit is heading for my lettuce patch. It eats every lettuce leaf it can find. What can I do? I don't have enough wire to put a fence around the whole garden."

"I can solve your problem, Grandpa," Dawn promised.

The next morning Grandpa found Dawn making a pile of pulled dandelions in a corner of the garden. "What are you doing out here so early?" he asked.

"I'm making dandelion salad for the bunny, Grandpa. You don't need the weeds, and the rabbits like these as much as lettuce."

1 The main characters are _____.

A Grandpa and the rabbit

B Grandpa and a gardener

C Dawn and Grandpa

D Dawn and a rabbit

2 The story happens _____.

F in an apartment building

G on a farm

H in a park

J in Grandpa's garden

3 The animal in the story is _____.

A Dawn's pet bunny

B a wild bunny

C Grandpa's pet bunny

D Grandpa's dog

4 The problem is that _____.

F Dawn doesn't help Grandpa

G Dawn doesn't like rabbits

H a rabbit is eating Grandpa's lettuce

J Grandpa grows too much lettuce

5 The problem is solved when _____.

A Dawn gathers dandelions for the rabbit to eat

B Grandpa builds a fence around the garden

C the rabbit eats the tomato plants

D Grandpa stops planting lettuce

```
Answers
1  Ⓐ  Ⓑ  © Ⓓ        4  Ⓕ  Ⓖ  Ⓗ  Ⓙ
2  Ⓕ  Ⓖ  Ⓗ  Ⓙ        5  Ⓐ  Ⓑ  ©  Ⓓ
3  Ⓐ  Ⓑ  ©  Ⓓ
```

Harcourt

Name _____

▶ Write two words from the cloud on each word line. Choose
one word with a milder meaning than the given word and
one word with a stronger meaning on each line. An example has been done
for you. Use each word only once.

cool	crave	enthusiastic	freezing	demand	hope
steal	blizzard	much	stormy	snowfall	content
take	suggest	cloudy	most		

MILDER WORD   **STRONGER WORD**

Example:

                    fair   good   great
    ←──→

1. ___content___   happy   ___enthusiastic___
    ←──→

2. ___suggest___   ask   ___demand___
    ←──→

3. ___cool___   cold   ___freezing___
    ←──→

4. ___hope___   want   ___crave___
    ←──→

5. ___cloudy___   rainy   ___stormy___
    ←──→

6. ___snowfall___   snowstorm   ___blizzard___
    ←──→

7. ___take___   remove   ___steal___
    ←──→

8. ___much___   more   ___most___
    ←──→

TRY THIS! Write a letter to the city council, describing your plan for a community
flower and vegetable garden. Use as many descriptive words as you can to
persuade the reader to use your garden design.

Harcourt

▶ **If the words form a sentence, write *sentence*. If not, think of words to make the sentence complete. Write the new sentence.**

1. Many people from the country.

   Responses will vary.

2. Made her uncle very happy.

   Responses will vary.

3. The cat slept on Lydia Grace's bed.

   sentence

4. She enjoys gardening.

   sentence

5. Uncle Jim's friend Emma.

   Responses will vary.

▶ **Rewrite these sentences. Begin and end them correctly.**

6. she planted seeds in cracked cups

   She planted seeds in cracked cups.

7. is her story a bit sad

   Is her story a bit sad?

8. the girl left her family behind

   The girl left her family behind.

9. did she move to a strange place

   Did she move to a strange place?

10. she seems very brave and clever

    She seems very brave and clever.

SCHOOL-HOME CONNECTION With your child, look at one or more letters from friends or family members. Notice what kinds of punctuation marks are used at the ends of sentences.

Harcourt

Name _____

▶ **Read this journal entry. Find and circle the twelve misspelled
words. Then write each word correctly on the lines below.**

We had a great time (palanting) our garden today. We
met at the empty lot. Some of us walked. Others came by
bus or (suwbay). The sky was (greay), but everyone felt
cheerful.

I'm afraid that bringing Ruff was a (misteak). He's a
sweet dog, but he loves to (scrach) and run. He even tried
to jump over the fence and (esceape). Liz grabbed him and
brought him (safly) back to me. I kept Ruff on his leash
(atfer) that. "Let's just hope the leash doesn't (braek)," said Liz.

The little kids (playd) while the rest of us dug holes
and dropped seeds into the ground. I had the (gratest) job
of all—using the hose to water the seeds.

When we finished planting, Ms. Kwan put a (stayk) and
some hot dogs on the grill, and we all had a terrific picnic.

SPELLING WORDS
1. played
2. escape
3. steak
4. subway
5. gray
6. safely
7. mistake
8. greatest
9. break
10. after
11. planting
12. scratch

1. _____planting_____   7. _____safely_____

2. _____subway_____   8. _____after_____

3. _____gray_____   9. _____break_____

4. _____mistake_____   10. _____played_____

5. _____scratch_____   11. _____greatest_____

6. _____escape_____   12. _____steak_____

Harcourt

Handwriting Tip: Use an overcurve stroke when joining a
letter to a circle-stroke letter. Write the Spelling Words below. — *ta*

13. escape _____escape_____   15. after _____after_____

14. greatest _____greatest_____   16. planting _____planting_____

Name _____

▶ **Write the word from above the jars. Read the word groups inside the jars. Then write the word that fits with each group.**

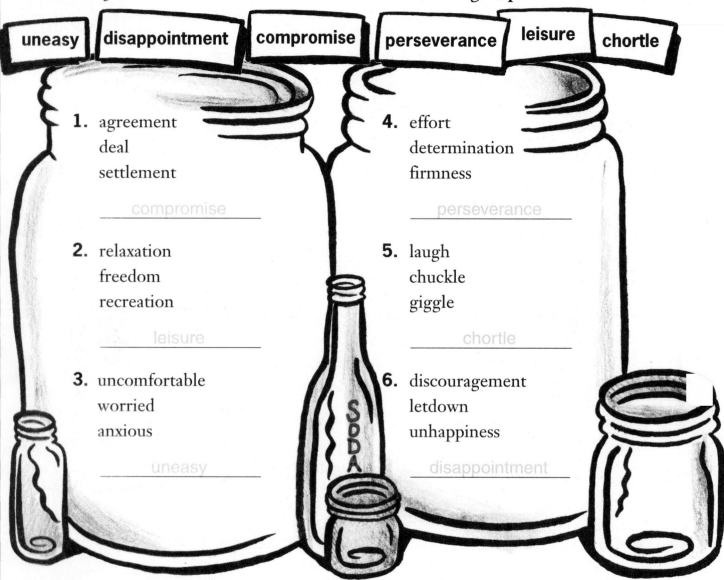

| uneasy | disappointment | compromise | perseverance | leisure | chortle |

1. agreement
   deal
   settlement

   compromise

2. relaxation
   freedom
   recreation

   leisure

3. uncomfortable
   worried
   anxious

   uneasy

4. effort
   determination
   firmness

   perseverance

5. laugh
   chuckle
   giggle

   chortle

6. discouragement
   letdown
   unhappiness

   disappointment

▶ **Write a Vocabulary Word that means the *opposite* of each word below.**

7. satisfaction   _disappointment_

8. calm   _uneasy_

9. surrender   _perseverance_

10. cry   _chortle_

TRY THIS! Describe a character from a favorite book or a cartoon series. Write three or four sentences, using at least three Vocabulary Words.

Harcourt

Name _____

Skill Reminder characters + setting + plot (problem, events, solution) = narrative elements

▶ **Read this play. Then write the correct phrase or phrases from the boxes to complete each sentence.**

MR. EDWARDS: Welcome to Edwards Antiques Emporium.

RACHEL: My great-grandmother is having a birthday party next week on September 30.

MR. EDWARDS: What kind of party are you having?

RACHEL: It's a costume party, and that's why I need clothes like people wore when Gran was young. Do you sell any antique clothing?

MR. EDWARDS: You've come to the right place! I've got old clothes for sale.

it is a costume party
Edwards Antiques Emporium
Rachel
Mr. Edwards sells
old clothes

Mr. Edwards
September
is having a birthday party
Rachel needs
old-fashioned clothes

The play takes place in the month of **(1)** _____ September _____

at **(2)** _____ Edwards Antiques Emporium _____. The characters

are **(3)** _____ Mr. Edwards _____ and

(4) _____ Rachel _____. Rachel's great-grandmother

(5) _____ is having a birthday party _____. The problem is,

(6) _____ Rachel needs old-fashioned clothes _____ because

(7) _____ it is a costume party _____. The problem is solved

because **(8)** _____ Mr. Edwards sells old clothes _____.

Name _____

▶ **Complete the story map below.** Possible responses are given.

Main Characters

Donavan Allen; Grandma;
residents in Grandma's apartment
building

Setting

Donavan's home; Grandma's
home; lounge of Grandma's
apartment building

Problem

Donavan has no more room in his word jar for words.

⇩

Important Events

Donavan takes his word jar to Grandma. He rejects her suggestion to trade
his words for something else. In the building lobby, he gives away a word
to two people who are arguing. Later he is upset to discover that other
people have taken all his words from the jar.

⇩

Solution

After Donavan sees how happy his words make the residents, he is
pleased that the words have been taken.

▶ **Write a one-sentence summary of the story's plot.**

Possible response: Donavan's word jar is full, and Donavan learns that

sharing his words by giving them to others makes them and him happy.

Harcourt

Name _____

▶ **Answer the questions. Write the answer on the line.**

Exact wording may vary.

"I'm off to Grandma's, off to Grandma's!" Merilee sang as she tossed clothes into her suitcase.

"Oh, Merilee," Mom sighed. "Your clothes will be all wrinkled if you pack them like that. Slow down and fold them carefully."

"I'll try, but I'm so excited!" Merilee answered. "I'll miss you and Dad, but it's always so much fun at Grandma's. We do such exciting things. Last year she took me to a wildlife farm, and we got to feed an antelope. The year before that Grandma and I went on an overnight trail ride. Neither one of us had ever been on a horse before, but we loved the ride. We said it was an adventure."

1. Does Merilee feel glad or sad about going to Grandma's? _____ glad _____

2. How do you know? She sings as she packs, and she talks about how
much fun she and Grandma always have.

3. Which of these words describes Merilee's character traits: *fearful, calm,* or

excitable? _____ excitable _____

4. How can you tell? She packs quickly and carelessly; she talks excitedly
about her visits with Grandma.

5. Which of these words describes Grandma: *timid, active,* or *angry*?

_____ active _____

6. What actions helped you know this? She takes Merilee to interesting
places.

7. Which of these words describes Merilee's and Grandma's character traits:

boring, shy, or *adventurous*? _____ adventurous _____

8. How can you tell? They like to do unusual things; they ride horses and
think the ride is an adventure.

TRY THIS! Choose a character from a story you have read. List several words to describe the character's traits. Write reasons you chose those traits.

Harcourt

Name _____

Donavan's
Word Jar

Grammar:
Declarative and
Interrogative
Sentences

▶ **Label each sentence *declarative* or *interrogative*.**

1. Have you seen Donavan's words? _____ interrogative _____

2. He loves the English language. _____ declarative _____

3. His collection is remarkable. _____ declarative _____

4. Can you define that word? _____ interrogative _____

5. I do not know its meaning. _____ declarative _____

▶ **Rewrite these sentences. Add the correct end marks.**

6. Did you look up that word

   Did you look up that word? _____

7. Have I spelled it correctly

   Have I spelled it correctly? _____

8. I checked it in the dictionary

   I checked it in the dictionary. _____

9. It looks correct to me

   It looks correct to me. _____

10. How do you pronounce it

    How do you pronounce it? _____

bungalow   compromise   menagerie   stupendous

dubious   kaleidoscope   bouffant   juggernaut

TRY THIS! Choose two words from the boxes above. Use one word to write a declarative sentence. Use the other one to write an interrogative sentence. Use a dictionary if necessary.

Harcourt

Name _____

▶ **Write the Spelling Word that means the opposite of each word or phrase.**

1. west _____ east

2. awake _____ asleep

3. above _____ beneath

4. argue _____ agree

5. full _____ empty

6. giving away _____ keeping

SPELLING WORDS
1. asleep
2. empty
3. queen
4. deal
5. needed
6. spelling
7. east
8. feelings
9. tea
10. keeping
11. beneath
12. agree

▶ **Write a Spelling Word to complete the sentences.**

The **(7)** _____ queen lifted her cup and

asked for more **(8)** _____ tea. "My

(9) _____ feelings are hurt," she said. "Didn't

you see that I **(10)** _____ needed more to drink?"

"I'm sorry, Mom," said the prince. "I'm having a

great **(11)** _____ deal of trouble with my

homework. Will you help me with my

(12) _____ spelling?"

Handwriting Tip: Take care to leave enough space between letters. Do not crowd letters. Write the Spelling Words below.

We fell asleep.

13. needed _____ needed   **15.** feelings _____ feelings

14. spelling _____ spelling   **16.** asleep _____ asleep

Harcourt

Name _____

▶ **Read the words in the box. Then read the pairs of words or phrases on the curtains. Write the word from the box that fits with each pair.**

| restless | pageant | rehearsals | troublesome | tropical | attentively |

1. bothersome
   annoying

   _____

2. practice times
   preparations

   _____

3. thoughtfully
   with great interest

   _____

4. show
   performance

   _____

5. hot climate
   wet and humid

   _____

6. uneasy
   not still

   _____

▶ **Write a word from the box above to complete each analogy.**

7. *Game* is to *athletes* as _____ is to *actors*.

8. *Look* is to *closely* as *listen* is to _____.

9. *Glad* is to *happy* as *unpleasant* is to _____.

10. *Up* is to *down* as *arctic* is to _____.

11. *Practices* are to *performances* as _____ are to *plays*.

12. *Light* is to *heavy* as *calm* is to _____.

TRY THIS! Imagine you were going to be in a school pageant. Write about the things you'd like to do. Use at least three Vocabulary Words.

Harcourt

Name _____

My Name Is
María Isabel

Characters'
Feelings
and Actions

Social Studies

Skill Reminder **Note a character's actions to find out the person's feelings and character traits.**

▶ **Read Samuel's letter. Then choose the word or phrase from the box to best complete each sentence.**

friendly	invite Samuel's family	nervous	tries new foods
welcoming	closes her eyes	polite	smile at them

Dear Jaime,

   Last Friday we took a bus from San Juan in Puerto Rico. We headed way up into the mountains. The road was narrow and steep, and Mom shut her eyes when we went around the curves. When we arrived, the whole town was celebrating its special day. The people had cooked festive foods, and there was singing and dancing. Some of the dishes seemed a little strange to me, but I ate a few bites of everything, because I didn't want to seem rude. All the people I met smiled at us and invited us to stay with them. See you soon!

                                   Your friend,
                                   Samuel

Readers know that the people in the town are **(1)** _____

and **(2)** _____. They **(3)** _____

to stay, and they **(4)** _____. Readers know that

Samuel's mother is **(5)** _____ because she

(6) _____ around the road's curves. Readers

know that Samuel is **(7)** _____ because he

(8) _____.

TRY THIS! List your own character traits. Give reasons for your description.

Harcourt

► As you read the story, fill in the prediction chart by writing what you think will happen. After you read, write what actually happens. Possible responses are given.

What I Predict Will Happen	What Actually Happens
María Isabel will tell her parents she's not in the pageant.	María Isabel does not tell her parents she is not in the pageant.
María Isabel will speak with her teacher about her problem.	María Isabel writes an essay for her teacher that explains her problem.
María Isabel will perform in the pageant.	María Isabel sings the Hanukkah song in the pageant.

► Write a one-sentence summary telling how María Isabel solved her problem.

Possible response: She writes how she feels in an essay to her teacher.

_____

Harcourt

Name _____

▶ Add a prefix or a suffix from the charts to each underlined word to make a new word that fits the definition. Write the new word on the line.

Prefix	Meaning
un-	not
re-	again
over-	too much
mis-	wrong
dis-	the opposite of

Suffix	Meaning
-less	without
-ous	full of
-ance	the act of
-able	capable of
-ly	in a certain way

1. to <u>spell</u> wrong _____

2. when you <u>perform</u> _____

3. not <u>prepared</u> _____

4. in a <u>clear</u> way _____

5. full of <u>humor</u> _____

6. to <u>write</u> again _____

7. to <u>eat</u> too much _____

8. without <u>hope</u> _____

9. able to be <u>read</u> _____

10. the opposite of <u>respect</u> _____

TRY THIS! Add a prefix or a suffix from the chart to each of these words: *wrap, commit, cheer, do, lead, help.* You may use the same prefix or suffix more than once. Use each word in a sentence.

Harcourt

Name _____

▶ **Read each sentence. Choose the answer that tells what the underlined word means. Mark the letter for that answer.**

1 If you do <u>badly</u> on the quiz, be sure to study hard for the test.

   A less bad

   B in a bad way

   C not bad

   D bad again

2 We were <u>misinformed</u> about what time the game would start.

   F given correct information

   G given too much information

   H given information again

   J given wrong information

3 It is <u>improper</u> to talk during the movie.

   A not proper

   B in a proper way

   C being too proper

   D less proper

4 He was <u>unsure</u> of the answer.

   F more than sure

   G not sure

   H capable of being sure

   J too sure

5 The <u>fearless</u> bird flew very high.

   A full of fear

   B capable of fear

   C without fear

   D the act of having fear

6 Don't throw a <u>breakable</u> glass.

   F capable of being broken

   G full of broken glass

   H not able to be broken

   J without being broken

7 The mountain goat climbed over the <u>dangerous</u> path.

   A full of danger

   B without danger

   C the act of finding danger

   D able to handle danger

8 I'll <u>refill</u> your glass with fresh water.

   F not fill

   G fill again

   H make half full

   J make too full

Answers

1 Ⓐ Ⓑ Ⓒ Ⓓ   5 Ⓐ Ⓑ Ⓒ Ⓓ

2 Ⓕ Ⓖ Ⓗ Ⓙ   6 Ⓕ Ⓖ Ⓗ Ⓙ

3 Ⓐ Ⓑ Ⓒ Ⓓ   7 Ⓐ Ⓑ Ⓒ Ⓓ

4 Ⓕ Ⓖ Ⓗ Ⓙ   8 Ⓕ Ⓖ Ⓗ Ⓙ

Harcourt

Name _____

▶ **Look at the picture of the school library. On each line, write the name of the section of the library that is the best place to find that item.**

1. an encyclopedia article about Mexico _____ reference books

2. a book of holiday poems _____ poetry

3. the names of all the books about Hanukkah _____ card catalog

   or _____ computer database

4. the novel called *In the Year of the Boar and Jackie Robinson* _____ fiction

5. a biography of Roberto Clemente _____ nonfiction

6. the names of all the books written by Gary Soto _____ card catalog

   or _____ computer database

7. the meaning of the word *diffident* _____ reference books

8. a map of Puerto Rico _____ reference books

9. a book of short stories _____ fiction

10. a copy of the latest issue of *National Geographic World* _____ magazines

Harcourt

Name _____

▶ **Write the answers to the questions on the lines. For questions 4–8, use the information on the cards from the card catalog and the computer database.**

Computer Database

```
11 OCT 01  GRANT COVE SCHOOL LIBRARY   2:03 pm
CALL NUMBER            JUNIOR FICTION, STACK D
        J FIC LOR              Status: Checked In
AUTHOR    Lord, Bette Bao
TITLE     In the Year of the Boar and Jackie Robinson /
          Bette Bao Lord; illustrations by Marc Simont.
EDITION   1st ed.
PUBLISHER New York, N.Y.: Harper & Row, c1984.
DESCRIPT  169 p.: ill.; 22 cm.
SUMMARY   In 1947, a Chinese child comes to Brooklyn,
          where she becomes
                         —More on Next Screen—
Press <Enter> to see next screen: O=Start Over, B=Back,
RW=Related Works, PH=Place Hold, C=Copy Status,
SB=Save Bib, <Enter>=Next Screen, SBLIST=Saved Bib List
```

Card Catalog

	In the Year of the Boar and Jackie Robinson
J	In the Year of the Boar and Jackie
Fic	Robinson / Bette Bao Lord; illustrations by
Lor	Marc Simont. 1st ed. New York, N.Y.: Harper
	& Row, c1984.
	169 p.: ill.; 22 cm.
	In 1947, a Chinese child comes to Brooklyn where
	she becomes Americanized at school, in her
	apartment building, and by her love for baseball.

1. Which of these sources of information probably takes up less space? _____computer database_____

2. For which kind must you use a keyboard? _____computer database_____

3. For which kind should you be familiar with the order of letters in the alphabet? _____card catalog_____

4. Who is the author of the book shown here? _____Bette Bao Lord_____

5. Who is the illustrator? _____Marc Simont_____

6. How many pages are in the book? _____169 pages_____

7. Is the book in the school library right now, or is it checked out? _____It is in the library._____

8. How do you know? _____The computer database screen shows "Checked In" next to the heading "Status."_____

SCHOOL-HOME CONNECTION Encourage your child to tell you about his or her school library. Ask what kinds of books the library has. Then ask your child to explain how he or she uses the card catalog or computer database to find a book.

Harcourt

Name _____

My Name Is
María Isabel

Grammar:
Imperative and
Exclamatory
Sentences

▶ **Label each sentence *imperative* or *exclamatory*.**

1. Wow, this song is difficult! _____exclamatory_____

2. Please play it one more time. _____imperative_____

3. What a nice tune it has! _____exclamatory_____

4. Listen to the low part. _____imperative_____

5. How lovely it sounds! _____exclamatory_____

▶ **Rewrite these sentences. Add the correct end marks.**

6. Sing the Hanukkah song again _Sing the Hanukkah song again._

_____

7. Tell us the story of Hanukkah _Tell us the story of Hanukkah._

_____

8. What an interesting story it is _What an interesting story it is!_

_____

9. Light the candles carefully _Light the candles carefully._

_____

10. How pretty they look _How pretty they look!_

_____

 TRY THIS! Write a paragraph about a holiday you love. Use all four kinds of sentences (declarative, interrogative, imperative, exclamatory).

Harcourt

Name _____

▶ **Write a Spelling Word to complete each sentence.**

1. Before we go to _____visit_____ Grandma, we'll buy you some new shoes.

2. Let's _____drive_____ to the shoe store.

3. We'll check to see if you need a larger _____size_____ now.

4. Which _____type_____ of shoe do you like—casual or dressy?

5. Do you want shoes that slip on or shoes that _____tie_____?

6. I can tell by your _____smile_____ that those are the shoes you want.

SPELLING WORDS
1. mine
2. tie
3. wild
4. type
5. smile
6. drive
7. size
8. blind
9. visit
10. thick
11. die
12. prize

▶ **Write the Spelling Word that rhymes with each word below.**

7. stick _____thick_____

8. nine _____mine_____

9. sigh _____die_____

10. tries _____prize_____

11. child _____wild_____

12. kind _____blind_____

Handwriting Tip: Be careful not to loop the letter *i*. Otherwise, it might look like an *e*. Write the Spelling Words below.

13. smile _____smile_____

14. visit _____visit_____

15. tie _____tie_____

16. prize _____prize_____

Harcourt

Name _____

▶ **Write the word from the box that matches each definition.
Two words will be used twice.**

immigrants	salary	modest	valuable
appreciation	courageous	tremendous	sportsmanship

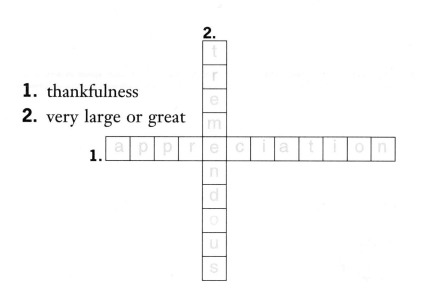

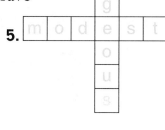

1. thankfulness
2. very large or great

2. t r e m e n d o u s
1. a p p r e c i a t i o n

5. not boastful
6. brave

6. c o u r a g e o u s
5. m o d e s t

3. people who come from
another country
4. behavior in a game

4. s p o r t s m a n s h i p
3. i m m i g r a n t s

7. gratefulness
8. money earned

8. s a l a r y
7. a p p r e c i a t i o n

9. money paid
for work
10. worth a lot

10. v a l u a b l e
9. s a l a r y

SCHOOL-HOME CONNECTION With your child, talk about people in
sports, politics, or entertainment whom you admire. Write a list of the
reasons you like each one. Use at least three Vocabulary Words.

Touch a Dream **23**

Name _____

| Skill Reminder | prefix + base word = new word |
| | base word + suffix = new word |

▶ Read the news article and write the word that best fits each definition in parentheses. Choose from the words in the box and add the correct prefix or suffix.

Prefix:	dis-	pre-	in-	im-			
Suffix:	-al	-ful	-ly	-ous	-less	-ty	
Words:	capable	help		possible	quick	courage	
	pleased	arranged		loyal	nation	hand	

NEW YORK, New York. October 20, 1957—Now that the 1957 season has ended, it is **(1) (not possible)**

_____impossible_____ to find more than one major league baseball team whose home is New York City. For years the Yankees, Dodgers, and Giants have fought for the **(2) (quality of**

being loyal) _____loyalty_____ of New York fans. Now only the Yankees will remain. Many baseball fans are **(3) (not capable)**

_____incapable_____ of understanding why the Giants and Dodgers have moved to California. To a **(4) (amount that fills a hand)**

_____handful_____ of New York fans, this is a **(5) (having courage)**

_____courageous_____ step to give baseball lovers in the West a chance to watch the **(6) (having to do with the**

nation) _____national_____ pastime. However, many others are **(7) (the opposite of pleased)**

_____displeased_____ with the owners' decision to take their much-loved teams away, but they are **(8) (lacking help)**

_____helpless_____ to do anything about it. Fans in Los Angeles and San Francisco have **(9) (arranged**

in advance) _____prearranged_____ celebrations to welcome their new teams, and officials are sure that baseball will **(10) (in a quick way)**

_____quickly_____ become even more popular in California.

Harcourt

Name _____

▶ Fill in the first two columns of the K-W-L chart. Then use information from the story to fill in the last column. Possible responses are given.

K	W	L
What I Know	**What I Want to Know**	**What I Learned**
Lou Gehrig was a famous baseball player.	Why was Lou Gehrig lucky?	Lou Gehrig did not miss a game in fourteen years. Lou Gehrig was selected as the American League's Most Valuable Player twice. He was shy and modest. When he became sick, the whole city honored him as a good sportsman and a good citizen. Lou Gehrig died at age thirty-seven.

▶ List five reasons why Lou Gehrig was admired both as a player and as a person by so many fans. Possible responses are given.

1. He played in 2,130 games in a row. _____

2. He never bragged about himself. _____

3. He was Most Valuable Player in 1927 and 1936. _____

4. He never complained about being ill. _____

5. He always showed good sportsmanship. _____

Name _____

▶ **Write the word identification strategy you used from the list in the box to figure out the meaning of each underlined word in the paragraph.** Responses may vary. Possible responses are given.

- **Think about the sounds the letters represent.**
- **Look for familiar word parts or for shorter words inside a longer word.**
- **Look for familiar patterns of letters in parts of the word.**
- **Blend sounds at the beginning of the word with vowel patterns.**
- **Look for spelling patterns.**
- **See if other words give clues about the word's meaning.**

Dizzy Dean was a <u>renowned</u> pitcher of the 1930s, who enjoyed a <u>sensational</u> career. In the Army, he was <u>required</u> to peel potatoes. He used the <u>spuds</u> as baseballs to practice his pitching. Later, as a <u>spectacularly</u> successful pitcher in the major leagues, Dizzy was known for his <u>unrestrained</u> boasts. <u>Prior</u> to the 1934 season, he said he would win more than 20 games. Everyone smiled and <u>chuckled</u>, but Dizzy won 30 games.

1. renowned _Look for familiar patterns of letters in parts of the word._

2. sensational _Look for familiar word parts or for shorter words inside a longer word._

3. required _Look for familiar patterns of letters in parts of the word._

4. spuds _See if other words give clues about the word's meaning; Look for spelling patterns._

5. spectacularly _Think about the sounds the letters represent._

6. chuckled _Blend sounds at the beginning of the word with vowel patterns._

Harcourt

SCHOOL-HOME CONNECTION With your child, start a list of interesting or unfamiliar words that you find in print. Ask your child to tell how he or she figures out how to pronounce or figure out the meanings of new words.

▶ **Write a compound word by using two of the three words given. An example has been done for you.**

Example:

basket	team	ball	basketball
1. team	base	mate	teammate
2. race	ball	track	racetrack
3. field	out	base	outfield
4. keeper	team	goal	goalkeeper
5. base	track	ball	baseball
6. foot	basket	race	footrace
7. board	basket	score	scoreboard
8. trap	park	ball	ballpark
9. play	hit	base	base hit
10. ball	high	fly	fly ball
11. play	game	double	double play
12. field	run	home	home run

 TRY THIS! Write down all the sport terms you can think of that are compound words, such as *racquetball* and *tennis ball*. Use a dictionary if necessary.

Harcourt

Name _____

Lou Gehrig

Grammar: Subjects and Predicates

▶ **Draw one line under each subject. Draw two lines under each predicate.**

1. I visited the Baseball Hall of Fame.

2. The museum has pictures of Lou Gehrig.

3. Some pictures show Babe Ruth, too.

4. Cooperstown is a wonderful place.

5. Many schoolchildren travel to the museum.

▶ **Add a subject or a predicate to complete each sentence.**
Responses will vary.

6. This baseball team _____.

7. _____ caught the ball.

8. _____ threw it to second base.

9. The runner _____.

10. _____ cheered in the stands.

TRY THIS!   Write five sentences about a sport you like. Draw one line under the subject and two lines under the predicate in each sentence you write.

28   Touch a Dream

Harcourt

Name _____

▶ **Use the Spelling Words and the clues below to complete the puzzle.**

Across

1. the person who helps team players
2. the month after May
3. opposite of *minus*
4. music
5. firm
6. knocked into pieces

Down

7. opposite of *sinking*
8. not these, but ____
9. a group of workers on a ship
10. disturbed
11. perform surgery
12. opposite of *leave out*

SPELLING WORDS

1. *those*
2. *coach*
3. *solid*
4. *include*
5. *crew*
6. *plus*
7. *operate*
8. *broke*
9. *upset*
10. *tune*
11. *June*
12. *floating*

Handwriting Tip: Make sure your letters sit evenly on the lower writing line. Write the Spelling Words below.

coach

13. tune _____   15. upset _____

14. June _____   16. plus _____

SCHOOL-HOME CONNECTION With your child, think of words that are related to baseball that have long or short *o* or *u* in them, such as *home run*.

Touch a Dream   29

Harcourt

Name _____

▶ **Write the word from the box that matches each definition.**

| earnestly | blizzard | frantically | stagger | scoured | bustled |

1. in a wild and excited way _____ frantically _____

2. hurried busily _____ bustled _____

3. a snowstorm _____ blizzard _____

4. in a serious way _____ earnestly _____

5. to walk in an unsteady way _____ stagger _____

6. rubbed and scraped _____ scoured _____

▶ **Write a word from the box to complete each sentence.**

Once the girls realized that the **(7)** _____ blizzard _____ had

snowed them in, they tried **(8)** _____ frantically _____ to get the

door open. When that didn't work, they **(9)** _____ bustled _____
about to find tools they might be able to use. They noticed the

storm had **(10)** _____ scoured _____ the windowpane and
the glass looked cracked. Then they phoned for help and believed

(11) _____ earnestly _____ that they would be rescued. After some

time, they saw someone carrying a shovel **(12)** _____ stagger _____
toward the house. Help had arrived.

SCHOOL-HOME CONNECTION With your child, talk about
a situation that calls for quick-thinking action. Use at least two
Vocabulary Words.

Harcourt

Name _____

▶ **Complete the cause-and-effect fishbone.**
Possible responses are given.

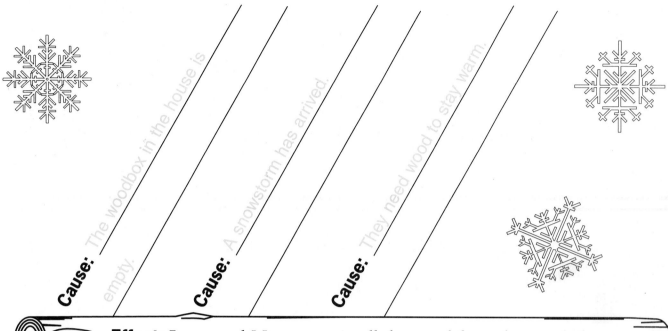

Cause: The woodbox in the house is empty.

Cause: A snowstorm has arrived.

Cause: They need wood to stay warm.

Effect: Laura and Mary carry in all the wood from the woodpile.

Cause: They don't want to burn furniture.

Cause: Their parents aren't there to do the job.

Cause: They don't know how much wood they will need.

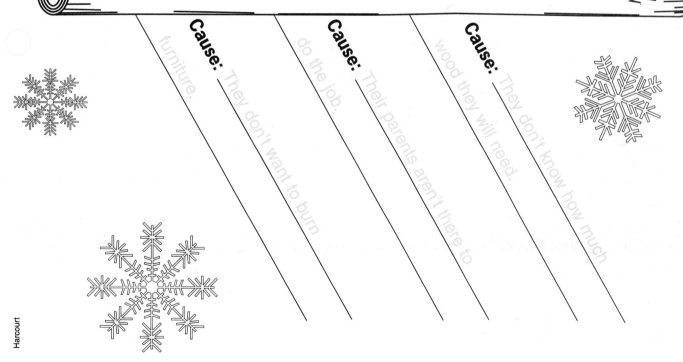

▶ **What does the girls' experience teach them and their parents?**

Possible response: The girls are able to make important decisions by

themselves in an emergency.

Harcourt

Name _____

▶ Below each want ad, write *first person* or *third person* to indicate the point of view. Then write two pronouns from the ad that helped you know.

NEEDED: STRONG PERSON to chop wood for my fireplace. I will provide breakfast. See Walter at the General Store after 8:00 A.M.

1. Point of view: _____first person_____

2. Pronouns: _____my, I_____

JOB OPEN NOW for patient person to train my dog. I expect gentleness and respect. See Mrs. Walker at the Post Office.

5. Point of view: _____first person_____

6. Pronouns: _____my, I_____

WANTED! Teacher for one-room school. Townspeople will pay well for a good teacher for their children. They offer free room and board. See Mayor Robinson.

3. Point of view: _____third person_____

4. Pronouns: _____their, they_____

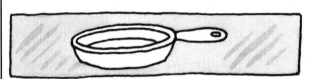

GOOD COOK NEEDED NOW for single homesteader. He is hungry for home cooking! Work in his kitchen for a good salary. See Henry one mile south of town.

7. Point of view: _____third person_____

8. Pronouns: _____he, his_____

HIRED HAND needed for our farm. We need help planting crops. See Mr. Fuller any time.

9. Point of view: _____first person_____

10. Pronouns: _____our, we_____

Harcourt

Name _____

▶ **Rewrite each want ad from page 32. Use the other point of
view. For example, if the ad was written in the first-person
point of view, rewrite it in the third-person point of view.**
Wording may vary but should include all points from the ads on page 32.

1. NEEDED: STRONG PERSON to
chop wood for Walter's fireplace.
He will provide breakfast. See
Walter at the General Store after
8:00 A.M.

3. JOB OPEN NOW for patient
person to train Mrs. Walker's dog.
She expects gentleness and
respect. See Mrs. Walker at the
Post Office.

2. WANTED! Teacher for one-room
school. Townspeople will pay well
for a good teacher for our
children. We offer free room and
board. See Mayor Robinson.

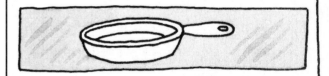

4. GOOD COOK NEEDED NOW
for single homesteader. I am
hungry for home cooking! Work
in my kitchen for a good salary.
See Henry one mile south of
town.

5. HIRED HAND needed for Mr.   planting crops. See Mr. Fuller
Fuller's farm. He needs help   any time.

Harcourt

Name _____

On the Banks of
Plum Creek

Grammar:
Complete and
Simple Subjects

▶ **Draw one line under each complete subject. Then circle each simple subject.**

1. Little Laura swept the floor.

2. Her sister cleared the table.

3. The two girls washed the dishes.

4. Their house seemed very quiet.

5. Every chore was finished.

▶ **Add a complete subject to complete each sentence.
Circle each simple subject.** Responses will vary.

6. _____ set the table.

7. _____ lay on the tablecloth.

8. _____ came out of the oven.

9. _____ smelled delicious.

10. _____ tasted wonderful.

11. _____ sat down.

12. _____ passed the bread.

TRY THIS! Write five sentences about doing household chores. Circle the simple subject of each sentence.

Harcourt

▶ **The letters of the underlined words are mixed up. Write the correct Spelling Words on the lines.**

1. One <u>nnftarooe</u>, Pa and I went walking in the woods. _____ *afternoon*

2. I saw a <u>unddwoe</u> squirrel. _____ *wounded*

3. "Who would <u>ohost</u> such a cute animal?" I wondered. _____ *shoot*

4. Its fur is <u>oomsht</u> and shiny. _____ *smooth*

5. "I'll <u>sobot</u> myself up so I can see," Pa said. _____ *boost*

6. The squirrel is <u>ingloof</u> us! _____ *fooling*

7. That put me in a good <u>omdo</u>. _____ *mood*

1. *hoop*
2. *wounded*
3. *shoot*
4. *booth*
5. *broom*
6. *boost*
7. *mood*
8. *fooling*
9. *afternoon*
10. *spoon*
11. *smooth*
12. *tooth*

▶ **Write the Spelling Word that names each picture.**

8.  _____ *spoon*

9. _____ *tooth*

10. _____ *booth*

11. _____ *broom*

12. _____ *hoop*

Handwriting Tip: Make sure your letters are not too light or too dark. Make them smooth and even. Write the Spelling Words below.

13. shoot _____ *shoot*

14. boost _____ *boost*

15. smooth _____ *smooth*

16. fooling _____ *fooling*

SCHOOL-HOME CONNECTION With your child, think of words that sound like *boot*. Then try to use as many of these words as you can in a short story.

Harcourt

Name _____

The Seven
Children

Vocabulary

► **Finish each sentence with a word from the box. Use each word twice.**

anticipation	unfamiliar	thicket	clearing	unity

1. I love hiking, dad. I'm bursting with
_____anticipation_____!

2. The trees are so close together in this
_____thicket_____.
I hope we don't get lost.

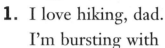

3. I'm _____unfamiliar_____ with this part of the woods.

4. Family, let's stay together. Remember the importance of
_____unity_____.

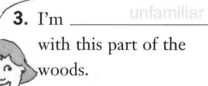

5. We'll have to help each other find a way through the
_____thicket_____ of trees.

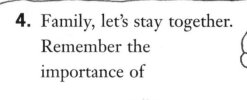

6. I see a
_____clearing_____
where some trees have been cut down.

7. I brought food for lunch and an umbrella in
_____anticipation_____ of rain.

8. We should check the map. This area looks _____unfamiliar_____ to me.

9. When we get into the open
_____clearing_____,
let's stop to eat and check our directions.

10. We'll work together. With
_____unity_____, I
know we'll be okay.

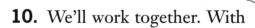

TRY THIS! Write a set of directions for someone hiking in the woods. Use at least two Vocabulary Words.

36 Touch a Dream

Name _____

▶ Complete the Venn diagram below by telling how the seven children behave at the beginning and at the end of the story. Then write ways the children behave that stay the same through the whole story. Possible responses are given.

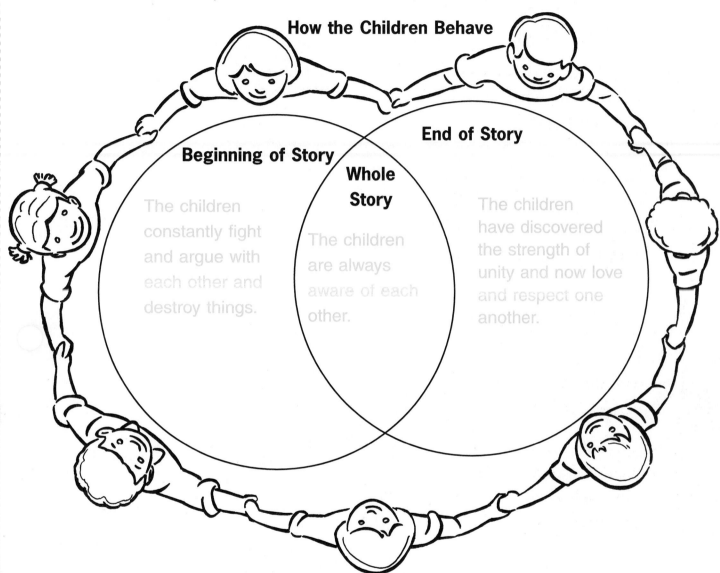

How the Children Behave

Beginning of Story

The children constantly fight and argue with each other and destroy things.

Whole Story

The children are always aware of each other.

End of Story

The children have discovered the strength of unity and now love and respect one another.

▶ Briefly describe how the children learn the value of unity.

Possible response: The father leaves the children in a strange part of the forest. Each child has been given a bundle. The contents of each bundle is useless without the other bundles. The children need each other. They are forced to cooperate in order to survive and to find their way home.

Harcourt

Name _____

▶ **Read the title and each part of the story. Then use story clues and what you already know to answer each question.**
Exact wording may vary.

The Three Foolish Woodsmen and the Donkey: A Fable

Once upon a time there were three men who worked in the forest. They gathered fallen logs and cut them into firewood. "Let's take our wood into the village to sell," said the first man. "We can each carry some," said the second. "No, only you two can carry the wood," said the third man. "I must lead our donkey."

"You are right," said the other two men, as each took a huge load of wood into his arms and began to walk down the long path. The third man led the donkey.

"We must stop and rest," panted the first woodsman.

"Yes," agreed the second, dropping his load of wood.

"I am not tired at all," said the third. "We must hurry on to the village so we can sell our wood before the sun goes down." The men began to argue. The donkey brayed and pawed the ground. Suddenly an old woman appeared beside them on the path.

"All three of you are silly," she said. "There's no need to argue. I can tell you what to do to solve your problem."

1. Is the story fiction or nonfiction? _____ fiction _____

2. What makes you think that? _____ It is a fable, and fables are fiction. _____

3. How will the two men who are carrying the wood soon feel? _____ very tired _____

4. What makes you think that? They are carrying heavy loads of _____

wood, and this is tiring. _____

5. How do you think the third man feels? not as tired as the other two _____

6. What do you think the woman will tell the men to do to solve their problem?

Let the donkey carry the wood. _____

7. What makes you think that? Donkeys are good at carrying loads. _____

8. Do you think the men will follow the old woman's advice? Why?

Answers will vary. _____

Harcourt

Name _____

▶ **Read each story. Then read each question and choose the
best answer. Mark the letter for that answer.**

Kami and her cousins wanted
to feed the birds that lived in
Kami's backyard. "We have some
birdseed and pine cones," Kami
said. "If we can make the seeds
stick to the pine cones, we can
hang them in the tree. Then the
birds can get to them." Two-year-
old Tommy looked up from his
snack. His fingers were covered
with peanut butter.

"I have an idea!" Kami cried.

1 The children will probably _____.

Ⓐ eat some peanut butter

Ⓑ scatter the seeds on the ground

Ⓒ use peanut butter to make the
seeds stick

Ⓓ ask Tommy to make the bird feeders

2 Which will they probably *not* do?

Ⓕ make bird feeders

Ⓖ use the pine cones and peanut butter

Ⓗ throw away the peanut butter

Ⓙ find a way to feed the birds

3 The leader will probably be _____.

Ⓐ Tommy

Ⓑ one of Kami's cousins

Ⓒ a friend

Ⓓ Kami

After a while the children were
hungry. Kami said they were out of
peanut butter, but she saw some
bread and cheese in the house.

4 The children will probably _____.

Ⓕ buy more peanut butter

Ⓖ eat nothing

Ⓗ make cheese sandwiches

Ⓙ wait until evening to eat

The next day Kami's dad hung
bird feeders in the tree. Then he
called Kami to the window.

5 Kami will probably see _____.

Ⓐ some birds in the tree

Ⓑ no birds at all

Ⓒ the bird feeders on the ground

Ⓓ cheese sandwiches

6 Which will the birds probably
not do?

Ⓕ enjoy the new bird feeders

Ⓖ fly away without eating

Ⓗ come back often to the tree

Ⓙ eat the birdseed

Harcourt

Name _____

▶ **Read the story below. For each underlined word, write the
homophone that fits the sentence. (Homophones are words
that sound alike but have different meanings and spellings.)**

Today I **(1)** <u>herd</u> the most amazing **(2)** <u>tail</u>. It was about a young girl who
lived by the ocean. She loved to fish. Each day, when the **(3)** <u>tied</u> came in, she
dropped her nets in the water.

Late one **(4)** <u>knight</u> she pulled out a very large fish. She was happy because
she knew she could sell it and **(5)** <u>by</u> a new comb for her **(6)** <u>hare</u>. Then the fish
started to talk.

"Where are you taking me?" asked the fish. The girl didn't know what to say.
Then the fish said, "Can we wait for a while? It is only one more **(7)** <u>our</u> until
(8) <u>mourning</u>, and I want to see the sun rise one more time. Then I will go with
you to the market."

What could the girl do? She put the fish in a bucket of water and sat down to
(9) <u>weight</u> for the sunrise. Soon she fell asleep. Do you **(10)** <u>no</u> what happened?
When she woke up, the tide had gone out. The fish was nowhere to **(11)** <u>bee</u>
found. He was far, far **(12)** <u>aweigh</u>.

1. ____heard____   5. ____buy____   9. ____wait____

2. ____tale____   6. ____hair____   10. ____know____

3. ____tide____   7. ____hour____   11. ____be____

4. ____night____   8. ____morning____   12. ____away____

 TRY THIS! Think of three pairs of homophones different from the ones shown above.
Then use each one in a sentence.

Harcourt

Name _____

▶ **Draw two lines under the complete predicate. Then circle the simple predicate.**

1. The oldest child (found) two flint stones.

2. One child (unfolded) a large quilt.

3. The youngest child (screamed) in terror.

4. The others (ran) to his side.

5. All of the children (shared) their stories.

▶ **Add a complete predicate to each subject. Circle the simple predicate in each complete predicate you write.** Responses will vary.

6. The campfire _____.

7. Water from the canteen _____.

8. Banana bread _____.

9. The map _____.

10. All seven children _____.

11. Their father _____.

12. The family _____.

 TRY THIS! Write four sentences giving examples of people helping each other. Circle the simple predicate in each sentence you write.

Harcourt

Name _____

▶ **Write a Spelling Word to complete each sentence. Use the picture clues.**

1. It _____barked_____ all night long.

2. Its _____alarm_____ will wake you up.

3. A turkey needs to be _____carved_____.

4. Get set to _____charge_____!

5. We _____parked_____ in the garage.

SPELLING WORDS

1. carved
2. garden
3. harm
4. farther
5. barked
6. alarm
7. chart
8. starved
9. harder
10. parked
11. smartest
12. charge

▶ **Write the Spelling Word that fits each clue.**

6. opposite of *softer* _____harder_____

7. at a greater distance _____farther_____

8. a diagram _____chart_____

9. cleverest _____smartest_____

10. hurt _____harm_____

11. suffered from hunger _____starved_____

12. seeds and flowers _____garden_____

Handwriting Tip: Close the letter *a* at the top. Do not loop the downstroke, or the *a* could look like *cl*. Write the Spelling Words below.

a

13. carved _____carved_____   15. alarm _____alarm_____

14. barked _____barked_____   16. harder _____harder_____

SCHOOL-HOME CONNECTION With your child, think of other words with the /är/ sound. Then use them in a story.

Harcourt

Name _____

▶ **Read the words on the flowers. Then write the word that answers each riddle. Use each word twice.**

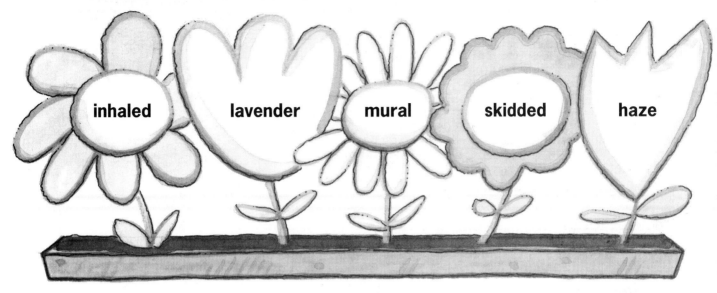

inhaled   lavender   mural   skidded   haze

1. I am a shade of purple.
   What color am I?   lavender

2. I was running fast. When I stopped
   quickly, I slid. What did I do?   skidded

3. I did this when I took air into my body.
   What did I do?   inhaled

4. I can make it hard to see.
   What am I?   haze

5. I am a very large picture made by
   one or more artists. What am I?   mural

6. I am like a fog.
   What am I?   haze

7. I'm a plant as well as a color.
   What am I?   lavender

8. I mean "breathed in."
   What word am I?   inhaled

9. I am art that is painted on a wall.
   What am I?   mural

10. When I stopped my bike, I left tire
    marks on the road. What did I do?   skidded

SCHOOL-HOME CONNECTION With your child, make up riddles
about items in your home. Use some Vocabulary Words in your
riddles. For example, "I smell like lavender. You put me on your
skin. What am I?" Guess the answers to each other's riddles.

Name _____

| Skill Reminder | your knowledge and experience + story clues = your prediction |

▶ **Read each story part. Then complete each sentence.**
Exact wording may vary.

"That blank brick wall on the back of our school isn't very pretty," Mr. Bromley said. "I wonder if there's anything we can do about it."

"Our art class has been looking for a project to do this year," said Luis.

1. The art class will probably _____ decorate the wall _____.

2. That is my prediction because art students can plan a creative decoration

for a wall, and the class needs a project to do _____.

On Wednesday, Luis said, "Tomorrow and Friday are school holidays for spring break. Let's start painting tomorrow."

"I'm busy tomorrow," said Alicia. "How about waiting until Friday to paint?"

"I heard something about rain that day," said Mr. Bromley.

3. The class will probably start painting on _____ Thursday _____.

4. That is my prediction because it is likely to rain on Friday, and the rain

would spoil the fresh paint _____.

The students worked hard all day and finished their painting.

"Let's plan a picnic for Saturday to celebrate," Mr. Bromley said.

"That's a great idea," agreed Luis. "Should we have the picnic in the morning or in the afternoon?"

5. The students will probably plan to have their picnic in the _____ afternoon _____.

6. That is my prediction because people don't usually eat breakfast at a

picnic, so picnics are held in the afternoon _____.

TRY THIS!   What do you predict the students will do if it rains on Saturday afternoon?

Harcourt

Name _____

▶ As you read, start to fill in the prediction web. After you
read, write what actually happens. Possible responses are given.

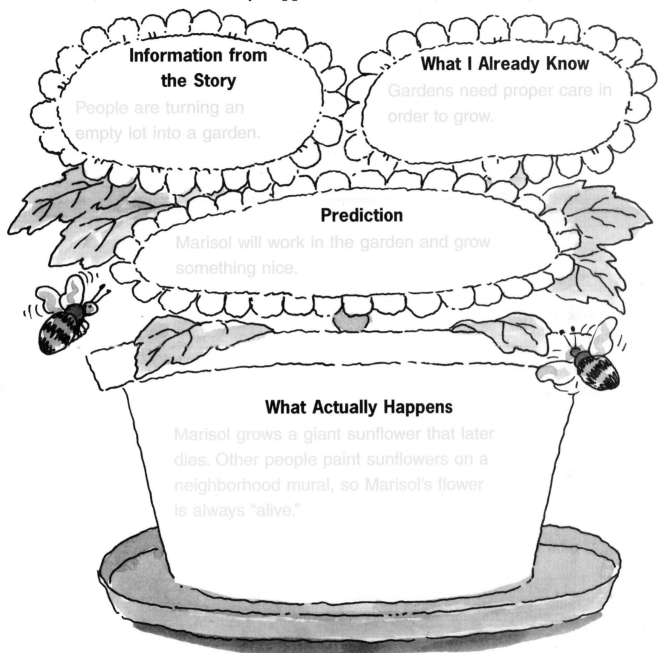

**Information from
the Story**

People are turning an
empty lot into a garden.

What I Already Know

Gardens need proper care in
order to grow.

Prediction

Marisol will work in the garden and grow
something nice.

What Actually Happens

Marisol grows a giant sunflower that later
dies. Other people paint sunflowers on a
neighborhood mural, so Marisol's flower
is always "alive."

▶ **Describe Marisol's problems and solutions.**

Possible responses: She has no seeds or space to grow anything, but

then she finds a seed and a tiny place to plant it. Marisol is sad that her

flower dies, but then she is cheered by a large mural of sunflowers that is

painted for her.

Harcourt

Name _____

▶ **Read each example of figurative language. Then write what each sentence means from the choices given.**

1. Mrs. Garza's flower garden was like a box of crayons.

   The garden was _____ very colorful _____.

   very colorful   **made of wax**   **square-shaped**

2. Mr. Potter's cornstalks marched from one end of the garden to the other.

   The cornstalks _____ stood in long rows _____.

   walked   **were in a parade**   **stood in long rows**

3. Looking at her own garden, Larissa's face was one big question mark.

   Larissa's face _____ showed she was puzzled _____.

   was sad   **was pear-shaped**   **showed she was puzzled**

4. Her tomato plants were flinging green arms everywhere.

   Her tomato plants _____ were growing everywhere _____.

   were green   **had sprouted arms**   **were growing everywhere**

5. Larissa put on her thinking cap and figured out what was wrong.

   Larissa _____ thought hard _____.

   wore a hat   **thought hard**   **designed a cap**

6. "I need to give those plants a hand," she said.

   She needed to _____ help the plants _____.

   help the plants   **water the plants**   **clap for the plants**

7. Larissa put a wire cage around each plant, so it could touch the sky.

   She helped each plant _____ grow tall _____.

   grow branches   **grow tall**   **grow into the clouds**

8. "Our gardens are our grocery stores," Mrs. Garza said.

   The gardens _____ provide food _____.

   are marketplaces   **provide food**   **grow inside stores**

SCHOOL-HOME CONNECTION With your child, listen for examples of figurative language you hear in everyday speech, on television, and on the radio. Start a list. Work with your child to write the real meaning next to each phrase.

Harcourt

The Garden of
Happiness

Grammar:
Compound
Subjects and
Predicates

Name _____

▶ **Draw one line under each simple subject.**
Draw two lines under each simple predicate.
Label each sentence *compound subject* **or** *compound predicate*.

1. Marisol and her friends worked. _____ compound subject _____

2. They weeded and hoed. _____ compound predicate _____

3. The garden blossomed and grew. _____ compound predicate _____

4. That man or his wife watered the plants.

_____ compound subject _____

5. He, she, and I picked beans. _____ compound subject _____

6. The hose twists, turns, and sprays the plants.

_____ compound predicate _____

▶ **Rewrite these sentences. Add commas where they are needed.**

7. The beans tomatoes and greens are ready to pick. _____

The beans, tomatoes, and greens are ready to pick. _____

8. Teenagers children and their parents watch. _____

Teenagers, children, and their parents watch. _____

9. We sprinkle soak or splash the vegetables. _____

We sprinkle, soak, or splash the vegetables. _____

10. Did Marisol Mr. Ortiz or Mr. Singh see the butterfly? _____

Did Marisol, Mr. Ortiz, or Mr. Singh see the butterfly? _____

TRY THIS! Write two sentences about gardening. Write one sentence with a compound subject and one with a compound predicate.

Harcourt

Touch a Dream   **47**

Name _____

▶ Read this newspaper article. Find and circle the twelve misspelled words. Then write each word correctly on the lines below.

Three murals went on display today at Day School. Students worked in groups to plan and paint them.

One mural's theme is *space*. Against a deep blue background, planets orbet the sun. Light seems to poar from the sun, our sourse of light and heat here on Earth.

Another group chose *spourts* for its mural's theme. A player throws a basketball fourward toward the hoop to scoar. A teammate, sidelined with a soir knee, cheers. The team has on uniforms players woer years ago.

The third mural's theme is *work* and shows how people suport themselves. It shows workers using machines to forse huge rocks out of the way. Other people bring oardar to a littered street.

Please, go and see the murals for yurself.

SPELLING WORDS

1. pour
2. orbit
3. score
4. source
5. sports
6. forward
7. force
8. order
9. wore
10. yourself
11. support
12. sore

1. _____orbit_____   7. _____sore_____

2. _____pour_____   8. _____wore_____

3. _____source_____   9. _____support_____

4. _____sports_____   10. _____force_____

5. _____forward_____   11. _____order_____

6. _____score_____   12. _____yourself_____

Handwriting Tip: When you write the *r* in the letter combination *or*, be careful to curve up and slant down. Otherwise, the letters *or* might look like *oi*. Write the Spelling Words below.

13. orbit _____orbit_____   15. order _____order_____

14. sports _____sports_____   16. support _____support_____

Harcourt

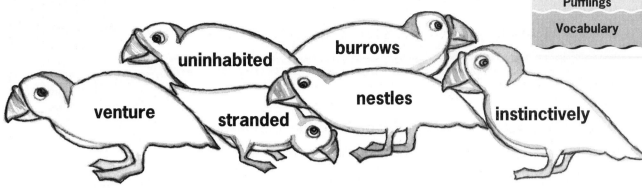

uninhabited

burrows

venture

stranded

nestles

instinctively

▶ **Write the word from above that matches each definition.**

1. left alone   _____ stranded _____

2. by nature   _____ instinctively _____

3. to travel at some risk   _____ venture _____

4. snuggles   _____ nestles _____

5. not lived in by anyone   _____ uninhabited _____

6. holes dug in the ground   _____ burrows _____

▶ **Write the Vocabulary Word that best completes each sentence.**

Rabbits live in **(7)** _____ burrows _____ they dig in the ground.

Sometimes other creatures **(8)** _____ venture _____ inside these holes,

not knowing whether they are already occupied or **(9)** _____ uninhabited _____.
One time my brother stepped in one of these holes and couldn't get his foot out.

He was **(10)** _____ stranded _____ until my father found him and got him
out. My brother is afraid of getting stuck again, so wherever he walks in our yard,

he now **(11)** _____ instinctively _____ watches for holes. We know that in our

yard, many a rabbit family **(12)** _____ nestles _____ beneath our feet.

TRY THIS! Imagine you are a puffling trying to fly for the first time. Write sentences
that tell what it feels like. Use at least two Vocabulary Words.

Harcourt

Name _____

| **Skill Reminder** | Use sounds, letter patterns, spelling patterns, and context clues to help you figure out new words. |

Science

▶ Write the strategy you used from the list below to figure out the meaning of each underlined word.

Responses may vary. Possible responses are given.

- **Think about the sounds the letters represent.**
- **Look for familiar word parts or shorter words inside a longer word.**
- **Look for familiar patterns of letters in parts of the word.**
- **Look for spelling patterns.**
- **See if other words give clues about the word's meaning.**

1. <u>Geothermal</u> energy under the earth's surface is used to heat homes in Iceland. See if other words give clues about the word's meaning.

2. This is heat that is <u>generated</u> inside the earth. Think about the sounds the letters represent.

3. Sometimes <u>magma</u>, or melted rock, lies near the surface of the earth. See if other words give clues about the word's meaning.

4. Rocks around the magma heat the <u>groundwater</u>. Look for familiar word parts or shorter words inside a longer word.

5. In Iceland the heated water is <u>transported</u> to homes through pipes. Look for familiar patterns of letters in parts of the word.

6. Iceland is known for its <u>geysers</u>, which are hot springs where steam and water shoot up. See if other words give clues about the word's meaning.

7. Old Faithful erupts on <u>schedule</u> about every 50 to 100 minutes. Look for spelling patterns.

Harcourt

▶ **Fill in the first two columns of the K-W-L chart. Then use information from the story to fill in the third column.**
Possible responses are given.

K	W	L
What I <u>K</u>now	**What I <u>W</u>ant to Know**	**What I <u>L</u>earned**
Puffins are sea birds.	Why do they come ashore and what are pufflings?	Puffins come ashore to lay their eggs. Pufflings are baby puffins.
Many birds migrate.	Where do Puffins make their nests?	In underground burrows.
Puffins stay awake during the day.	What is going to happen to the pufflings at night?	When grown, they will try to fly to sea.
It is hard to see at night.	How can the pufflings be helped?	The children have flashlights and rescue the pufflings. They release the birds by the shore the next day.

▶ **Write a one-sentence summary of the whole selection.**

Possible response: Each year in August, children in Iceland rescue pufflings

on land and help launch them out to sea.

Name _____

▶ **Read the story. Then write the correct causes and effects
to complete the chart.**

"Cheep! Tweet!" It was only a tiny sound, but it caused Patrick to stop his
bike and look under the bush. There he found a little bird. It tried
to fly away when it saw Patrick, but one of its wings was injured.
Since Patrick didn't know what to do to help the bird, he dashed
up the sidewalk and rang the doorbell at Mr. Grant's house.

"Mr. Grant, can you help? You know a lot about birds, and I've found
one that has a hurt wing," Patrick said. Mr. Grant got gloves, a small box
with air holes and a cover, and a small towel, and he followed Patrick to
the bush. He carefully picked up the injured bird and put it into the box.

"You were right to call me," Mr. Grant said. "People shouldn't try to
care for wild creatures at home, so we'll take it to the Wildlife Rescue
Center where I work." At the center, the manager told Patrick, "Because
you were careful and gentle, this bird will soon be as strong as ever.
She will fly again."

Exact wording will vary but should include these causes and effects.

Causes	Effects
Because Patrick heard a noise,	he **(1)** stopped his bike and **(2)** looked under the bush.
Finding the bird caused Patrick to	**(3)** run to Mr. Grant's house and **(4)** ask Mr. Grant to help.
Because people shouldn't **(5)** care for wild creatures at home,	Mr. Grant and Patrick **(6)** took the bird to the Wildlife Rescue Center.
Since Patrick was **(7)** careful and **(8)** gentle with the bird,	the bird will soon be **(9)** as strong as ever and will be **(10)** flying again.

Harcourt

Name _____

▶ **Read the passage. Then read each question and choose the best answer. Mark the letter for that answer.**

Hundreds of years ago huge sheets of ice called *glaciers* covered a small island called Iceland. When the big glaciers melted, lake-sized chunks of ice stayed buried in the ground. After a time, these chunks melted and left holes in the ground that eventually filled with water. That is why present-day Iceland is dotted with lakes.

Only a small part of Iceland can be used for farming, so many Icelanders make their living by fishing. Since the growing season is short, Icelanders use greenhouses to grow vegetables and fruit indoors.

Although Iceland's climate is cool, people swim outdoors in hot springs where the water is warmed.

Iceland is called the Land of Frost and Fire because it has both warm places—hot springs—and cold places—glaciers.

1 Many of Iceland's lakes were created by _____.

 A hot springs

 B glaciers

 C rushing streams

 D ponds

2 Because Iceland has so little farm land, _____.

 F there is not enough to eat

 G people grow their own food

 H many people make their living from the sea

 J people eat too much fish

3 People in Iceland use greenhouses because _____.

 A the growing season is short

 B they don't know much about farming

 C they have large backyards

 D the weather is hot

4 Because of hot springs, people in Iceland can _____.

 F swim in the ocean

 G swim only in the summer

 H swim outdoors in cool weather

 J eat more fish

5 Iceland is called the Land of Frost and Fire because it has _____.

 A summer and winter seasons

 B bonfires and icicles

 C stoves and refrigerators

 D hot springs and glaciers

Answers

1 Ⓐ Ⓑ Ⓒ Ⓓ

2 Ⓕ Ⓖ Ⓗ Ⓙ

3 Ⓐ Ⓑ Ⓒ Ⓓ

4 Ⓕ Ⓖ Ⓗ Ⓙ

5 Ⓐ Ⓑ Ⓒ Ⓓ

Harcourt

Name _____

► **Write the answer to each question on the line.**

Exact wording may vary.

1. If you wanted to find out how flamingoes care for their young, in which encyclopedia volume might you look? _____Volume F_____

2. After choosing the encyclopedia volume, what would you do? Use the guide words to find the article "flamingo."

3. After finding the correct article, how would you find the information you are looking for? Look at headings within the article to find the section about the bird's care of the young.

4. If you wanted to find the most recent list of endangered animals, would it be better to look in a print encyclopedia or on the Internet? on the Internet

   _____

5. Why? Many Web sites are updated often, so they usually have more current information than print encyclopedias have.

6. List three words separated by AND that you might use in a search for this information on the Internet. Any 3 of these possible responses: endangered, animals, species, conservation, protection, wildlife

7. After you type the search words, how do you get the computer to begin its search? Possible answer: Press the ENTER key, or click the mouse with the arrow on "search."

8. To find a list of endangered animals in the index of an encyclopedia, what entries might you look under? Possible responses: endangered, animals, species, conservation, protection, wildlife

Harcourt

Name _____

▶ **Write the key words you would use to perform a search on the Internet for the answer to each question.**

Answers may vary.

1. What birds live in a swamp?

_____ birds _____ AND _____ swamp _____

2. What kind of nest do ospreys build?

_____ osprey _____ AND _____ nest _____

3. What birds do you see in Texas?

_____ birds _____ AND _____ Texas _____

4. Where is the toucan's habitat?

_____ toucan _____ AND _____ habitat _____

5. What special care does a pet parakeet need?

_____ parakeet _____ AND _____ care _____

6. How do you train a parrot to talk?

_____ parrot _____ AND _____ training _____

7. What parrots are found in Africa?

_____ parrot _____ AND _____ Africa _____

8. What kinds of wildlife are found in Alaska?

_____ Alaska _____ AND _____ wildlife _____

9. What kind of woodpecker lives in a cactus plant?

_____ woodpecker _____ AND _____ cactus _____

10. Where do geese go when they migrate?

_____ geese _____ AND _____ migrate _____

▶ **Write a word from the box to complete each analogy. An example has been done for you.**

chick	puppy	lamb	duckling
pond	pen	field	barn

Example:

    Puffling is to *puffin* as _____cub_____ is to *bear*.

1. *Kitten* is to *cat* as _____lamb_____ is to *sheep*.

2. *Colt* is to *horse* as _____chick_____ is to *chicken*.

3. *Calf* is to *cow* as _____puppy_____ is to *dog*.

4. *Tadpole* is to *frog* as _____duckling_____ is to *duck*.

5. *Yard* is to *dog* as _____pen_____ is to *pig*.

6. *Desert* is to *coyote* as _____pond_____ is to *duck*.

7. *Den* is to *wolf* as _____barn_____ is to *cow*.

8. *Beach* is to *crab* as _____field_____ is to *sheep*.

TRY THIS! Make a list of some of your favorite wild animals. Use a science dictionary to find out what these animals are called when they are babies. For example, a baby seal is called a pup, just like a baby dog.

Harcourt

▶ **Identify each word group as a *comma splice* or *run-on sentence*. Then rewrite each one correctly as a compound sentence.**

1. Halla has a flashlight she carries a box. run-on sentence; Halla has a

   flashlight, and she carries a box.

2. The bird fell, Halla saved it. comma splice; The bird fell, but Halla saved it.

   _____

▶ **Rewrite each pair of sentences as a compound sentence, using the conjunction in parentheses ( ).**

3. The birds are slow. They move well in water. **(but)**

   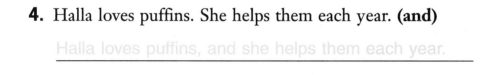
   The birds are slow, but they move well in water.

   _____

4. Halla loves puffins. She helps them each year. **(and)**

   Halla loves puffins, and she helps them each year.

   _____

5. Children climb the cliffs. They watch the puffins. **(and)**

   Children climb the cliffs, and they watch the puffins.

   _____

6. The puffins ignore them. They hide in holes. **(or)**

   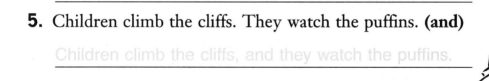
   The puffins ignore them, or they hide in holes.

   _____

TRY THIS! Write three compound sentences about an unusual animal. Use each of the conjunctions *and, or,* and *but* once.

Harcourt

Name _____

▶ **Use the Spelling Words and the clues below to complete the puzzle.**

Across
5. not often
6. felt brave enough
7. having to do with milk
8. looked hard

SPELLING WORDS
1. cared
2. dairy
3. unfair
4. rarely
5. stared
6. dared
7. glare
8. airplanes
9. barely
10. farewell
11. software
12. staircase

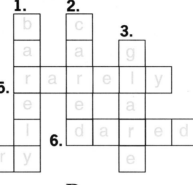
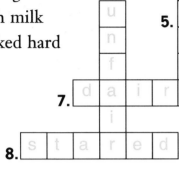

Down
1. only just
2. felt interested
3. a bright light
4. not right

▶ **Put a word from the first puffin together with a word from the second puffin. Write each Spelling Word you make.**

soft   fare
case   planes

stair   air
ware   well

9. _____ software _____   11. _____ staircase _____

10. _____ farewell _____   12. _____ airplanes _____

Handwriting Tip: Be sure to bring the downstroke of *a* to the bottom writing line, or it might look like an *o*. Write the Spelling Words below.

13. rarely _____ rarely _____   15. airplanes _____ airplanes _____

14. glare _____ glare _____   16. farewell _____ farewell _____

Harcourt

▶ Write the word from the web that matches each clue. Two
   words will be used twice.

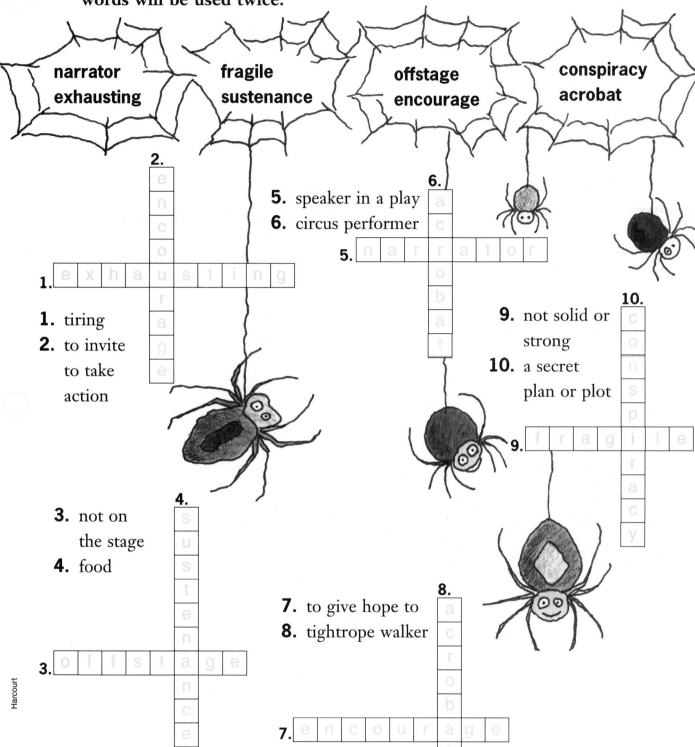

narrator
exhausting

fragile
sustenance

offstage
encourage

conspiracy
acrobat

5. speaker in a play
6. circus performer

1. tiring
2. to invite
   to take
   action

9. not solid or
   strong
10. a secret
   plan or plot

3. not on
   the stage
4. food

7. to give hope to
8. tightrope walker

2. encourage
1. exhausting
5. narrator
9. fragile
3. offstage
4. sustenance
7. encourage

TRY THIS! Imagine that you are an animal on the Zuckerman farm. Describe a typical
day. Use at least three Vocabulary Words.

Harcourt

Name _____

| **Skill Reminder** | cause = why something happens |
| | effect = what happens |

▶ **Read the passage. Then write four causes and their effects.**
Exact wording may vary.

The grass spider builds a special two-part web so it can get its food without leaving home. Here's how: the spider spins a tangle of "ropes" like a wall. Flying insects are stopped by the "ropes" and fall down. They land on a flat part of the web that the spider has woven across the branches of a bush or across a patch of grass. Since this part of the web is soft and bouncy, insects cannot move across it very well. Because the grass spider is able to zip across the web, it can reach its prey before the insect has a chance to escape. These webs are called funnel webs. Because funnel webs are thick and silky, people long ago used them as bandages.

1. **cause:** The grass spider builds a two-part web.

   effect: The grass spider can get its food without leaving home.

2. **cause:** Funnel webs are thick and silky.

   effect: People long ago used funnel webs as bandages.

3. **cause:** The spider is able to zip across the web.

   effect: It can reach its prey before the insect escapes.

4. **cause:** The spider spins a tangle of "ropes."

   effect: Flying bugs are stopped and fall onto the web below.

TRY THIS! Make a list of some causes and effects you know about insects. For example, because bees fly from flower to flower, they spread pollen.

Harcourt

Name _____

▶ **Complete the story map below.** Possible responses are given.

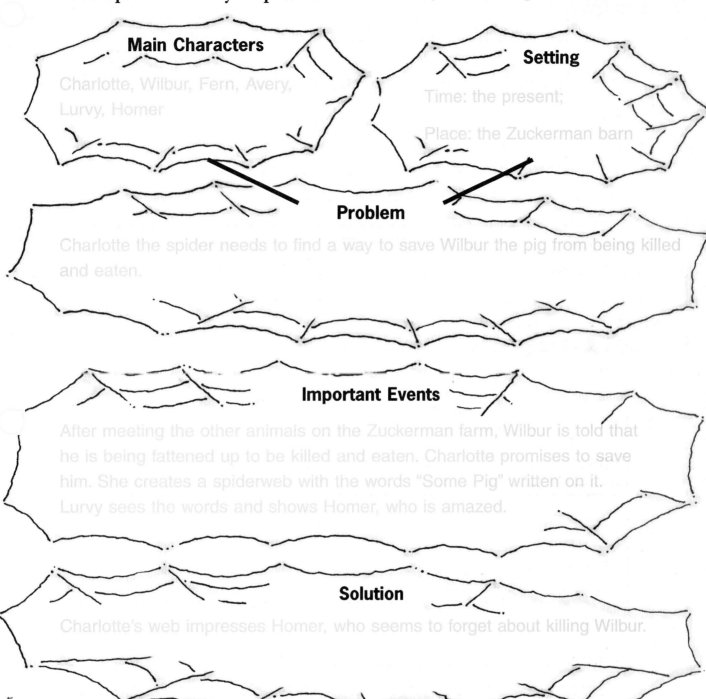

Main Characters

Charlotte, Wilbur, Fern, Avery, Lurvy, Homer

Setting

Time: the present;

Place: the Zuckerman barn

Problem

Charlotte the spider needs to find a way to save Wilbur the pig from being killed and eaten.

Important Events

After meeting the other animals on the Zuckerman farm, Wilbur is told that he is being fattened up to be killed and eaten. Charlotte promises to save him. She creates a spiderweb with the words "Some Pig" written on it. Lurvy sees the words and shows Homer, who is amazed.

Solution

Charlotte's web impresses Homer, who seems to forget about killing Wilbur.

Harcourt

▶ **Write a one-sentence summary describing the kind of personality Charlotte has. Base your answer on her words, thoughts, and actions.**

Possible response: She is a loving creature who sincerely cares about her

_____

fellow animals.

_____

Name _____

▶ **Write the theme that best fits each story summary.**

1. Joe dislikes spiders. He tries to keep them out of his vegetable garden. Then Joe learns that spiders can be helpful, because they eat harmful insects in the garden. He learns to tell the difference between harmful spiders and those that help. Joe decides that not all spiders are bad.

Theme: Don't make up your mind about a subject before you have all

the facts.

a. Don't make up your mind about a subject before you have all the facts.
b. Learn all you can about spiders before you plant a garden.
c. There are spiders that help and spiders that hurt.

2. LaShonda spends the summer on her aunt's farm. The aunt doesn't pay much attention to her neice. LaShonda helps during a storm and then gives her aunt a hug. Her aunt hugs her back and suggests that they bake cookies together.

Theme: Some people hide their feelings and are much nicer than they

seem.

a. Don't spend the summer with someone you don't know.
b. Relatives should take care of each other.
c. Some people hide their feelings and are much nicer than they seem.

3. Nathan and his older brother Lem are eight years apart in age and have very different interests. Lem mostly ignores Nathan and thinks of him as a little child. When a blizzard strikes their farm, Nathan and Lem have to work together and Lem discovers that Nathan can do hard jobs. At the end of the story, the brothers are playing a game together.

Theme: Working together can make people appreciate each other.

_____

a. Working together can make people appreciate each other.
b. Brothers who are far apart in age are seldom close.
c. Older brothers don't have much time for younger brothers.

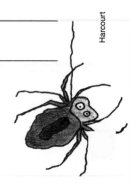

Harcourt

▶ **Write the theme that best fits each story summary.**

1. Every day Lucy rides her horse from her family's homestead to the one-room school on the prairie. One day there is a huge dust storm. Lucy can see only a few inches ahead, and she has no idea which way to go. Her horse knows the way, though, and takes her safely home.

   Theme: _Animals can be good friends to people._ _____

   _____

   a. Riding a horse to school can be dangerous.
   b. Animals can be good friends to people.
   c. Horses know how to navigate in the dark.

2. Sally takes care of the chickens on her family's farm. Her parents let her keep part of the money she makes from selling eggs. She saves her money and buys a fancy doll. After she buys it, fire destroys a neighbor's house. Sally thinks over an idea and then gives her new doll to the neighbor's daughter Caroline. Sally misses the doll, but she is glad to see Caroline's happy face.

   Theme: _Giving something away can bring a special kind of happiness._

   _____

   a. Giving something away can bring a special kind of happiness.
   b. You should save your money in case of emergencies.
   c. Don't save your money, because you may not keep what you buy with it.

3. When Hal visits his grandpa's farm, he is unhappy and embarrassed because he doesn't know anything about farm animals or crops. Hal is good at building and repairing things, though. When Grandpa's plow breaks, Hal is able to fix it. This makes him feel much better about himself.

   Theme: _All kinds of talents are useful._

   _____

   a. If you don't know something, it will be embarrassing.
   b. If you don't know about animals, learn to fix things.
   c. All kinds of talents are useful.

Harcourt

SCHOOL-HOME CONNECTION Discuss a story that both you and your child know. Ask your child to tell you what the story's theme is.

Name _____

▶ **Beside each dictionary definition below, write a related word from the box.**

salutations	congratulations	terrific	acrobat
miracle	sustenance	supreme	magazine

1. _____terrific_____ : *terrificus;* Latin for **frightened** or **excited**

2. _____salutations_____ : *salutare;* Latin for **to greet** or **to welcome**

3. _____acrobat_____ : *acrobate;* French for **a rope dancer**

4. _____sustenance_____ : *soutenir;* French for **to hold up**

5. _____congratulations_____ : *congratulatus;* Latin for **wished joy**

6. _____supreme_____ : *supremus;* Latin for **uppermost**

7. _____miracle_____ : *miraculum;* Latin for **a wonder** or **marvel**

8. _____magazines_____ : *makhazin;* Arabic for **storehouses**

acrobat!

 TRY THIS! Use a dictionary to find the origins of the following words: *encyclopedia, automobile, furniture.*

Harcourt

▶ **Find the independent and dependent clauses in these sentences. Draw one line under each independent clause. Draw two lines under each dependent clause.**

1. After the goose laid eight eggs, seven eggs hatched.

2. When Avery fought Fern, he broke an egg.

3. After the eggs hatched, the gander was proud.

4. The goose was very busy because she had goslings to take care of.

▶ **Rewrite each sentence. Add the kind of clause shown in parentheses ( ). Remember to add commas as needed.** Responses will vary.

5. Templeton took the egg _____. **(dependent)**

   _____

6. After the goose honked _____. **(independent)**

   _____

7. _____ because Fern tossed them some corn. **(independent)**

   _____

8. _____ the goose returned to her nest. **(dependent)**

   _____

TRY THIS! Write a paragraph telling what happens after the ending of "Charlotte's Web." Include dependent clauses in at least three sentences. Draw one line under the independent clauses and two lines under the dependent clauses in the sentences you write.

Harcourt

Name _____

▶ **Write a Spelling Word to complete each sentence.**

1. I _____search_____ for hidden spiderwebs.

2. I wonder how that spider _____learned_____ to make a web.

3. I admire each _____curve_____ in the web.

4. The spider seems to work hard, as if making a web were an _____urgent_____ task.

5. Spiders have taken the art of weaving _____further_____ than we can imagine.

6. That spider has _____earned_____ my admiration.

SPELLING WORDS
1. curve
2. learned
3. curly
4. pearl
5. purse
6. further
7. turtle
8. urgent
9. burning
10. search
11. earth
12. earned

▶ **Write a Spelling Word to complete the phrase about each picture.**

7. Aunt Jo's _____purse_____

8. a _____burning_____ candle

9. _____curly_____ hair

10. a _____pearl_____ necklace

11. our home, the _____earth_____

12. a _____turtle_____

Handwriting Tip: Bring the last downstroke of *u* to the bottom writing line, or it might look like *v*. Write the Spelling Words below.

13. curly _____curly_____

14. purse _____purse_____

15. turtle _____turtle_____

16. urgent _____urgent_____

Harcourt

► **Write the word from the tree top that matches each definition. The message in the shaded area beside the tree trunk tells you who hangs out in trees. Two words are used twice.**

| endangered | smuggled | jealous | manageable |
| displeasure | facial | coordination | |

1. angry that another has what you do not

2. disapproval

3. of the face

4. close to not existing anymore

5. able to be handled

6. taken secretly

7. the smooth movement of parts

8. unhappiness

9. able to be controlled

SCHOOL-HOME CONNECTION With your child, talk about ways people and animals interact. Use at least three Vocabulary Words.

Touch a Dream **67**

Name _____

▶ **Fill in the first two columns of the K-W-L chart. Then use
information from the story to fill in the last column.**
Possible responses are given.

K	W	L
What I Know	**What I Want to Know**	**What I Learned**
Orangutans are wild animals.	Why do humans babysit orangutans?	When mothers of young orangutans have been killed, the young apes can't survive alone in the jungle.
Some baby animals need help in order to survive.	How do you babysit an orangutan?	Orphan orangutans need a lot of care and help to become able to live in the forest.
It can be dangerous to live in the jungle.	How do humans and orangutans get along?	Orangutan babies are loving and loveable.

▶ **Make a list of five rules for babysitting a baby orangutan. Think about the
most important needs that an orangutan has.** Possible responses are given.

1. Give it milk twice a day.

2. Give it medicine baths to fight skin diseases.

3. Allow food snatching to help it recognize which foods are safe to eat.

4. Let it climb trees to build muscles and develop jungle skills.

5. Be prepared to let it go free after seven or eight years.

Harcourt

Name _____

▶ **Fill in the notepad with notes about each passage.** Responses
will vary but should include the ideas shown.

Notepad

1. Prairie dogs are social animals. This means that they live together in family groups. Prairie dogs live in underground "towns." Different family groups have their own "neighborhoods," with many different underground rooms connected by tunnels. Some rooms are for sleeping, and others are for storing food. Some are nurseries, where young prairie dogs are raised.

1. Prairie dogs live in family groups in underground towns. Their neighborhoods have rooms connected by tunnels. Different rooms are for sleeping, storing food, and raising the young.

2. Prairie dog "towns" include listening posts above ground. There, the animals listen for enemies. When a prairie dog hears an enemy, it barks to warn others to hide. This barking noise gave the prairie dog its name, but the animal isn't really a dog. It is a type of ground squirrel.

2. Prairie dogs listen for enemies at listening posts. They bark to warn other prairie dogs to hide. Because of the bark, they are called prairie dogs, but they are really ground squirrels.

3. Barking is just one of the sounds that prairie dogs make. Sometimes they stand on their hind legs, throw their heads back, and give a whistling call. They may be signaling that no enemies are in sight, or they may be letting other prairie dogs know that this is their territory. Prairie dogs may jump straight up while they are whistling, and sometimes they even fall over backward!

3. Sometimes prairie dogs make a whistling sound to signal that there are no enemies around or to show that this is their territory. They may jump straight up and even fall over backward.

Harcourt

Name _____

▶ **Fill in the notepad with notes about each passage.** Responses will vary but should include these ideas.

1. Underground prairie dog towns make good homes because they are cooler in summer and warmer in winter than the air above. Since the underground rooms are comfortable and safe, other animals make use of them.

2. Burrowing owls sometimes move into prairie dog holes. They make nests there, lay eggs, and hatch their young in a home they didn't even have to build! Burrowing owls may take over holes dug by other animals, too, such as badgers or skunks.

3. During hot weather, rattlesnakes often move into prairie dog burrows to keep cool. When this happens, the prairie dogs don't always move out. Instead, they may just build a wall between the snake's room and the rest of the burrow. Prairie dog burrows are popular with rattlesnakes during the winter, too. Dozens of them may hibernate in a cozy room.

Notepad

1. Prairie dog towns are cool in summer and warm in winter and are safe, so other animals also use the rooms.

2. Burrowing owls sometimes make nests, lay eggs, and hatch young in prairie dog holes. They may also take over other animals' homes.

3. Rattlesnakes may move into prairie dog burrows in the summer to keep cool. Then, rather than move out, the prairie dogs may wall off the snake's room. Dozens of the rattlesnakes may hibernate in a prairie dog burrow during the winter.

TRY THIS! Read a magazine or encyclopedia article about an animal that interests you. Take notes on the article so you can share the information with someone at home.

Harcourt

Name _____

▶ **Read the following paragraphs. Then complete the
outline below.** Exact wording may vary.

Many wild animals provide places for their babies to stay safe while
they are young and helpless. One kind of shelter is a hole or cave called a
den. Foxes dig dens. Their pups are born there and live there while they
are growing up. Wolves also dig dens, sometimes with the help of other
adult wolves in the pack. Coyotes use dens, too, but sometimes they take
over another animal's burrow and make it larger.

Some kinds of birds protect their young in tunnels. Atlantic puffins dig
into grassy land near the sea. Bee-eaters peck holes in a cliff and make
them larger until they have long tunnels. Kingfishers dig their tunnels in
the banks of streams.

Other birds make tree holes for their babies. Screech owls don't peck
out their own holes. Instead, they find a natural hollow spot in a tree or a
hole made by another bird. Woodpeckers make their own tree holes.

Shelters for Baby Animals

I. Dens

   A. Foxes _____

   B. Wolves _____

   C. Coyotes _____

II. Tunnels

   A. Atlantic puffins _____

   B. Bee-eaters _____

   C. Kingfishers _____

III. Tree holes

   A. Screech owls _____

      1. Don't make their own holes

      2. Use natural hollows or holes made by other birds _____

   B. Woodpeckers _____

Harcourt

▶ **Read the following paragraphs. Then complete the outline.**

Exact wording may vary.

Bird parents work hard to bring up their babies. Since many newly hatched birds have no feathers, the adult birds must keep the bodies of their young the right temperature. Parents huddle over the young birds to keep them warm when the weather is cool. In hot weather, they may spread their wings over the babies to give them shade.

Of course, parents must feed their babies. Baby birds eat quite often. Their parents make many trips back and forth to the nest, bringing food.

Another important job of the parents is to protect their young from danger. They may try to chase away a predator. At other times, they may try to distract the predator. To do this, they let the predator see the parent go in the opposite direction from the nest. Often, the parent will make itself look injured. All this display is to try to get the predator to follow the parent away from the baby birds.

Parents Bringing Up Baby Birds

I. Must keep them the right temperature

   A. Huddle over the babies to keep them warm

   B. Spread wings over them to keep them cool

II. Must feed them

   A. Babies eat quite often.

   B. Parents bring food to the nest.

III. Must keep them safe from danger

   A. Chase away an enemy

   B. Distract an enemy so it follows parent away from babies

      1. Let the enemy see the parent leaving the nest

      2. Make the enemy think the parent is injured

TRY THIS! Find and read an interesting nonfiction passage in a book or magazine in your classroom. Outline the article to help you remember the information. Start with the topic headings and add the details.

Harcourt

Name _____

▶ Label each sentence *simple,* *compound,* or *complex.*

1. Orangutans are sweet, but they have sharp

   teeth. _____compound_____

2. When I met Nanang, he

   was very young. _____complex_____

3. Nanang will return to the forest. _____simple_____

4. After he returns to the forest, my job is done.

   _____complex_____

▶ **Draw one line under each independent clause. Draw two lines
under each dependent clause.**

5. Since Nanang does not have his mother, he needs the babysitter.

6. Although he is young, he is quite strong.

▶ **Combine each pair of sentences into a complex sentence.
The connecting words in the box may help you.**
Responses will vary; possible responses are given.

after	because	since	when
although	before	if	while

7. Nanang held my hand. We walked in the forest.

   Nanang held my hand while we walked in the forest.

   _____

8. Nanang is so young. He is in danger from snakes.

   Because Nanang is so young, he is in danger from snakes.

   _____

SCHOOL-HOME CONNECTION Have your child write a short
paragraph about his or her different chores at home. The paragraph
should include at least two complex sentences.

Touch a Dream **73**

Harcourt

▶ **The letters of the underlined words are mixed up. Write the correct Spelling Words on the lines.**

1. The orangutans
   formed a <u>occunli</u>.   council

2. They sit on the <u>drgonu</u>.   ground

3. They talk <u>taoub</u>
   problems.   about

4. Does that <u>kcbagorudn</u>
   noise bother them?   background

5. They hold their
   next meeting in
   the city, <u>wwnndtoo</u>.   downtown

6. Then they can
   spread their papers
   out on a <u>treocnu</u>.   counter

SPELLING WORDS
1. ground
2. frown
3. downtown
4. bounced
5. council
6. about
7. scout
8. counter
9. background
10. amount
11. bound
12. shower

▶ **Write the Spelling Word that rhymes with each word below.**

7. sound   bound

8. shout   scout

9. pounced   bounced

10. town   frown

11. flower   shower

12. count   amount

Handwriting Tip: Make sure each letter is
the correct size. Similar kinds of letters should be
the same size. Write the Spelling Words below.

13. council _____ council _____   15. amount _____ amount _____

14. bound _____ bound _____   16. downtown _____ downtown _____

Harcourt

Name _____

▶ **Read the words in the box. Write the word that best completes each analogy.**

| alarmed | windbreak | conch | paddock | rustle |

1. *Apple* is to *fruit* as _____ conch _____ is to *seashell*.

2. *Happy* is to *pleased* as *frightened* is to _____ alarmed _____.

3. *Loud* is to *shout* as *soft* is to _____ rustle _____.

4. *Windshield* is to *glass* as _____ windbreak _____ is to *trees*.

5. *Pen* is to *pigs* as _____ paddock _____ is to *horses*.

▶ **Choose the word from the box above that matches each clue. Write the word in the puzzle.**

Down

6. a soft, whispering noise

7. a line of trees

8. a fenced field for horses

Across

9. frightened

10. a type of seashell

Harcourt

TRY THIS! Make a list of things you might see and do if you visited a farm or a beach. Use at least two Vocabulary Words.

Name _____

Skill Reminder	*I, me, we, us, our, ours, my, mine* = first person
	he, she, him, his, her, hers, they, them, their, theirs = third person

▶ Read each sentence and write *first person* or *third person* to tell the point of view. Then write one pronoun from the sentence that helped you identify the point of view.

When my family and I were pioneers in Nebraska, I went to a school built of bales of straw.

1. Point of view: _____first person_____

2. Pronoun clue: _____my or I_____

Our building didn't last long, because it caught fire late one night.

3. Point of view: _____first person_____

4. Pronoun clue: _____Our_____

Many pioneer families wanted their children to learn to read and write.

5. Point of view: _____third person_____

6. Pronoun clue: _____their_____

Students usually didn't have desks, and they sat on benches, not chairs.

7. Point of view: _____third person_____

8. Pronoun clue: _____they_____

We were often cold and uncomfortable, but we were glad for the chance to learn.

9. Point of view: _____first person_____

10. Pronoun clue: _____We_____

 TRY THIS! Look back at a story you have read this year. On a separate sheet of paper, write the story title. Then tell the point of view the writer used. List some clues that help you identify the point of view.

Harcourt

Name _____

▶ **Complete the character map below. Write important information about each of the characters.** Possible responses are given.

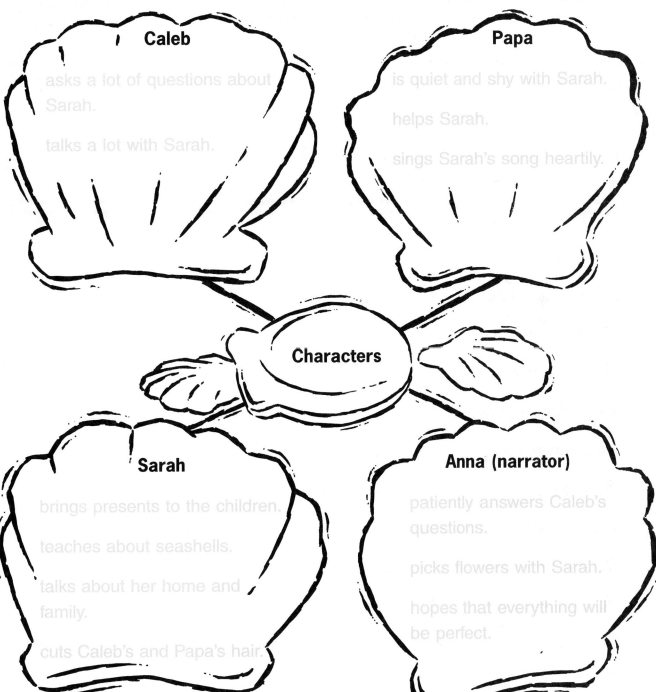

Caleb

asks a lot of questions about Sarah.

talks a lot with Sarah.

Papa

is quiet and shy with Sarah.

helps Sarah.

sings Sarah's song heartily.

Characters

Sarah

brings presents to the children.

teaches about seashells.

talks about her home and family.

cuts Caleb's and Papa's hair.

Anna (narrator)

patiently answers Caleb's questions.

picks flowers with Sarah.

hopes that everything will be perfect.

▶ **Write a one-sentence summary telling what effect Sarah has on the family.**

Possible response: She gives them hope that Papa will be happy, and she teaches them about a life they have never known.

Harcourt

Name _____

► Read each paragraph. Use information in the paragraph and your own knowledge to draw conclusions about the character. Then write the answer to each question.

Mindy wiggled her toes in the sand happily and looked out at the ocean. The cool breeze and warm sand made her smile. How much fun it was to splash in the water! She wished the day would never end.

1. Does Mindy like the beach? _____yes_____

► **List the clues that helped you draw this conclusion.**

Exact wording may vary.

2. She wiggles her toes in the sand happily.

3. She smiles and wishes the day would never end.

4. *Mindy wants to stay at the beach as long as possible.* Is this a valid conclusion?

Why? Yes. People behave this way when they are somewhere they like.

_____

Kelli hadn't smiled all day. "Why did we ever come to the beach?" she grumbled. "There's sand in my hair. There's even sand in my sandwich! Ugh!" She stayed under the beach umbrella and just took a nap.

5. Does Kelli like the beach? _____no_____

► **List the clues that helped you draw this conclusion.**

Exact wording may vary.

6. She complains about the sand.

7. She stays under the beach umbrella and takes a nap.

8. *Kelli wants to stay on the beach a long time.* Is this a valid conclusion? Why?

No. People behave this way when they are in a place they don't like.

_____

TRY THIS! Think about another story you have read this year that you enjoyed. What conclusion can you make about how one of the characters felt?

Harcourt

Name _____

▶ **Read the paragraph. Then choose the best answer for each question, and mark the letter for that answer.**

How can you build a house if you don't have any wood or bricks? In the early 1900s farmers in Nebraska used hay because it was easy to find. Machines pressed the dried hay and tied it into blocks called *bales*. These bales of hay were each about four feet long and two feet wide. With the help of their neighbors, farmers would stack the bales of hay to make walls. They knew that they could add wooden floors and shingle roofs later, when they might be able to get wood. Hay houses were fairly warm in winter, but people living in them had to be careful of fire, since hay burns easily. Hay walls were also good places for fleas to live.

1 Farmers in Nebraska grew _____.

A many fruit trees

B large oak trees

C a lot of hay

D no crops at all

2 What information helped you decide how to answer question 1?

F Farmers had so much hay that they could use it for building houses.

G There was plenty of fruit.

H There was plenty of wood.

J It took a long time to build a house.

3 Farmland in Nebraska had _____.

A many trees

B very few trees

C many brick factories

D not enough hay

4 What information helped you decide how to answer question 3?

F Bales of hay were very heavy.

G There weren't many bricks.

H Farmers ran out of hay.

J People didn't have enough wood to build houses.

5 Farmers in Nebraska in the early 1900s _____.

A always worked alone

B depended on neighbors for help

C had money to buy everything they wanted

D didn't get along with their neighbors

Answers
1 Ⓐ Ⓑ ● Ⓓ
2 ● Ⓖ Ⓗ Ⓙ
3 Ⓐ ● Ⓒ Ⓓ
4 Ⓕ Ⓖ Ⓗ ●
5 Ⓐ ● Ⓒ Ⓓ

Harcourt

Name _____

▶ **On each line, write the phrase that means the opposite of the underlined phrase in the sentence.**

1. When a new person came by, the kitten was <u>quiet and shy</u>.
   noisy and friendly   *OR*   **silent and meek**

   _____ noisy and friendly _____

2. Jack made a little clay bowl that was <u>round and perfect</u>.
   beautifully circular   *OR*   **lopsided and flawed**

   _____ lopsided and flawed _____

3. When Jenny finished washing and combing her hair, it was <u>straight and wet</u>.
   snarled and dry   *OR*   **shiny and slick**

   _____ snarled and dry _____

4. Rebecca wanted the <u>smoothest and whitest</u> piece of marble she could find.
   roughest and dirtiest   *OR*   **finest and clearest**

   _____ roughest and dirtiest _____

5. The creek water was <u>cool and sparkling</u> around Sarah's ankles.
   warm and dark   *OR*   **cold and bright**

   _____ warm and dark _____

6. When it came out of the dryer, the laundry was <u>warm and dry</u>.
   cool and damp   *OR*   **hot and fuzzy**

   _____ cool and damp _____

7. Jim's Grandma was always <u>calm and kind</u>.
   pleasant and nice   *OR*   **nervous and mean**

   _____ nervous and mean _____

8. The last piece of sandpaper left was <u>large and rough</u>.
   big and gritty   *OR*   **tiny and smooth**

   _____ tiny and smooth _____

TRY THIS! Write a short paragraph describing a place you would like to visit. Then use a thesaurus to find antonyms for each descriptive word. Use these words to write a paragraph describing a place you would never want to visit.

Harcourt

Name _____

▶ **Write *common* or *proper* to identify each underlined noun.**

1. The <u>sheep</u> ran in the field. _____common_____

2. As we waited, <u>Caleb</u> played with a marble. _____proper_____

3. Suddenly he saw a yellow <u>bonnet</u>. _____common_____

4. Papa's wagon was pulled by <u>Jack</u> and Old Bess. _____proper_____

5. Sarah brought <u>Seal</u>, a gray cat with white feet. _____proper_____

▶ **For each sentence, fill in the blank with a common noun.** Responses will vary. Possible responses are given.

6. We watched the wagon with _____hope_____ in our hearts.

7. The wagon passed the _____barn_____ and then stopped.

8. One of Sarah's gifts was a(n) _____shell_____.

9. Sarah told my _____brother_____, Caleb, about gulls.

10. Sarah's room had a(n) _____quilt_____ in it.

▶ **Complete each sentence by writing a proper noun in the blank.**
Responses will vary. Possible responses are given.

11. Before he left, _____Papa_____ combed his hair.

12. Sarah gave Caleb's sister, _____Anna_____, a sea stone.

13. Did the stone really come from the state of _____Maine_____?

14. Lottie and _____Nick_____ stared at Sarah's cat.

15. _____Seal_____ stepped out of her case and purred.

 TRY THIS! Write a paragraph about a time when someone visited your family. Use both common and proper nouns.

Harcourt

Name _____

▶ **Write the Spelling Word that fits each clue.**

1. This person could
   give you a job. _____ employer _____

2. It would make you
   very sick. _____ poison _____

3. It describes something
   ruined. _____ spoiled _____

4. Make decisions
   about these. _____ choices _____

5. When your friends
   speak, they use these. _____ voices _____

6. It describes an egg
   cooked in water. _____ boiled _____

SPELLING WORDS
1. boiled
2. annoyed
3. choices
4. poison
5. employer
6. joining
7. spoiled
8. voices
9. destroyed
10. pointing
11. avoided
12. enjoying

▶ **Write a Spelling Word to complete each sentence.**

Dad was **(7)** _____ annoyed _____ that it was raining.

It **(8)** _____ destroyed _____ his plans. He was

(9) _____ enjoying _____ his day off, but now he

(10) _____ avoided _____ anything outdoors. I was

(11) _____ pointing _____ to a video, hoping he

would be **(12)** _____ joining _____ me soon.

Handwriting Tip: When you join the letter *o* to
another letter, be sure to keep the joining stroke high.
Otherwise, the *o* might look like an *a*. Write the
Spelling Words below.

oi oy

13. annoyed _____ annoyed _____   15. spoiled _____ spoiled _____

14. pointing _____ pointing _____   16. enjoying _____ enjoying _____

Harcourt

Name _____

▶ **Use words from the boxes to complete the sentences in the story. Two words will be used twice.**

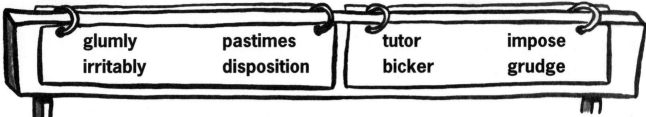

glumly pastimes
irritably disposition

tutor impose
bicker grudge

Bill's friend was late. Bill felt disappointed as he sat waiting

(1) _____ glumly _____ in front of the TV.

Just then his cousin, Dave, came in. He looked annoyed. "Two members of the Little League team have decided to take up soccer and tennis

as their **(2)** _____ pastimes _____ instead of baseball," Dave said

(3) _____ irritably _____. He asked Bill to play on the baseball team.

Bill began to **(4)** _____ bicker _____ with Dave and told him to leave

him alone. His normally happy **(5)** _____ disposition _____ was clouded because he was upset that his friend was late. Dave saw that Bill was in a bad mood.

He didn't want to **(6)** _____ impose _____, so he left.

But as he walked away, Dave felt he had better come to an understanding with Bill. He didn't want a senseless

(7) _____ grudge _____ to build up between them that would carry bad feelings. So he went back inside and asked Bill if there was a problem he could help with. Bill told him about his friend being late. Dave replied, "We can fix that. When he arrives,

we'll both **(8)** _____ tutor _____ him in how to tell time!"

Bill couldn't help but laugh. His cheerful **(9)** _____ disposition _____ showed again. He told Dave he would gladly consider baseball as one

of his **(10)** _____ pastimes _____.

TRY THIS! Think of another story you have read that involves a family situation. Describe the story, using at least three Vocabulary Words.

Harcourt

Name _____

Skill Reminder	clues in text + what you already know = conclusion

▶ **Read the sentences and write the correct conclusions on the lines. Then write about the clue that helped you.**

Exact wording may vary.

Marisa Hernández and her mother show their pet goat in competitions. Marisa's pets also include two dogs, a rabbit, a lamb, and a pony.

1. Which conclusion can you draw?
   a. Marisa likes goats better than lambs.
   b. Marisa likes many different kinds of animals.

   Marisa likes many different kinds of animals.

2. **Clue:** Marisa has many different pets.

Kevin Lockhart reads a story to his three-year-old sister, Ashley. "I want Ashley to learn to love books as much as I do," Kevin says.

3. Which conclusion can you draw?
   a. Kevin doesn't like to spend time with his sister.
   b. Kevin has learned that reading can be fun.

   Kevin has learned that reading can be fun.

4. **Clue:** Kevin says that he loves books.

Maylee Chen shows her prize-winning rock collection. It took Maylee three years to collect and identify all these rocks.

5. Which conclusion can you draw?
   a. Maylee runs out of patience in a hurry.
   b. Maylee sticks with a project once she starts it.

   Maylee sticks with a project once she starts it.

6. **Clue:** Maylee worked on her collection for three years.

TRY THIS! Make a list of conclusions you can draw about a person you know or a character you have read about.

Harcourt

Name _____

▶ **Complete the cause-and-effect fishbone.**
Possible responses are given.

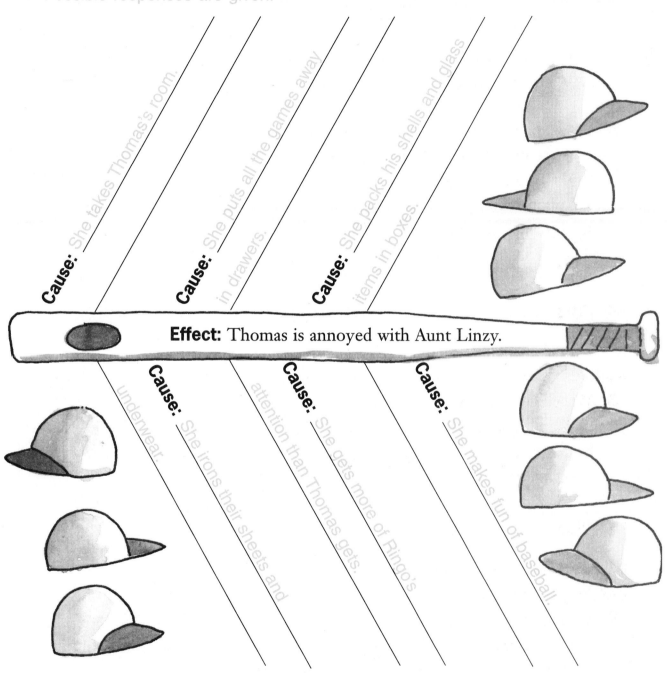

Cause: She takes Thomas's room.

Cause: She puts all the games away in drawers.

Cause: She packs his shells and glass items in boxes.

Effect: Thomas is annoyed with Aunt Linzy.

Cause: She irons their sheets and underwear.

Cause: She gets more of Ringo's attention than Thomas gets.

Cause: She makes fun of baseball.

▶ **Write a one-sentence summary telling how Grandfather's feelings about Aunt Linzy compare with Thomas's feelings.**

Possible response: Grandfather also gets annoyed with Aunt Linzy, but in

time he grows more used to her and is more understanding.

_____

Harcourt

Name _____

▶ **Read the passage. Then complete the chart to show five ways Derek and Kyle are alike and five ways they are different.**
Exact wording may vary.

Derek wasn't sure he wanted his cousin Kyle to spend the summer with him and his family. Both boys were baseball fans, but Derek cheered for the Pirates and Kyle was a fan of the Giants. Kyle didn't like cats, and Derek loved his pet kittens. "I talk a lot, and he's so quiet. He doesn't like to go to movies like I do. It's good that we both like to swim," Derek thought, "but I like to go out with Uncle Bill on his sailboat. Kyle doesn't know the first thing about sailing. We'll both enjoy eating the fish we catch, though."

"Both of you like to play soccer," Uncle Bill reminded Kyle. "You're both good at board games, too. I'll bet you'll have some fun together after all."

Ways Derek and Kyle Are Alike	Ways Derek and Kyle Are Different
1. Both are baseball fans.	6. Derek cheers for the Pirates, and Kyle is a Giants fan.
2. Both like to swim.	7. Kyle doesn't like cats, and Derek loves his pet kittens.
3. Both like to eat the fish they catch.	8. Derek talks a lot, and Kyle is quiet.
4. Both like to play soccer.	9. Derek likes to go to movies, and Kyle doesn't.
5. Both are good at board games.	10. Derek likes to go out on Uncle Bill's sailboat, and Kyle doesn't know anything about sailing.

SCHOOL-HOME CONNECTION Talk with your child about two places you have been, such as a park, store, or someone's home. Ask your child to list ways the two places are alike and different.

Harcourt

Name _____

Stealing Home

Extending
Vocabulary:
Figurative
Language/Simile

▶ **Write the simile from the box that best completes each sentence.**

like a baby	**like a fool**	**like whipped cream**
like the sun	**like trees**	**like best friends**
like a fish out of water	**like a freight train**	**like day and night**
like two peas in a pod		

1. The tornado was very loud. It sounded

_____ like a freight train _____.

2. I love to watch the clouds pile up on a summer day. They look

_____ like whipped cream _____.

3. My little brother says broccoli looks

_____ like trees _____.

4. Rick forgot his lines in the school play. He felt

_____ like a fool _____.

5. Rebecca's smiling face shines

_____ like the sun _____.

6. Abbey and Erica are sisters and do everything together.

They are _____ like best friends _____.

7. Julie felt very out of place at her new school.

She felt _____ like a fish out of water _____.

8. I went to bed the minute I got home from camping. I closed my

eyes and slept _____ like a baby _____.

9. The twins looked exactly alike and always
wanted to do the same things. They were

_____ like two peas in a pod _____.

10. He was outgoing and she was shy. They were

_____ like day and night _____.

▶ **Draw one line under each noun. Write *S* above each singular noun and *P* above each plural noun.**

           P   S   S

  1. All the shells and a special fossil were in a box.

               P   S

  2. Many other boxes were on the porch.

        S   S   P

  3. My aunt will buy a dresser for her belongings.

             P   S

  4. Do the animals like the new visitor?

       P   P

  5. The boys got on their bicycles and went

                  S

     for a long ride.

▶ **Replace each blank with the plural form of the word in parentheses ( ). Then rewrite each sentence.**

  6. The _____ finished the jigsaw puzzle. **(woman)** The women finished the

     jigsaw puzzle.

  7. "Baseball players earn big _____," Aunt Linzy said. **(salary)** "Baseball

     players earn big salaries," Aunt Linzy said.

  8. The guest did not want to catch _____. **(catfish)** The guest did not want

     to catch catfish.

  9. Did Aunt Linzy use _____ to cut vegetables? **(knife)** Did Aunt Linzy use

     knives to cut vegetables?

  10. When the _____ ran by, the cat showed its _____. **(mouse, tooth)** When

     the mice ran by, the cat showed its teeth.

Harcourt

SCHOOL-HOME CONNECTION Work with your child to make a list of fifteen nouns that name items found in the home. Write the singular and plural forms of each noun.

Name _____

▶ **Read this journal entry. Find and circle the twelve misspelled words. Then write the words correctly on the lines below.**

Meen, wimen, and children were at the fair. Everyone wore geans. In the cooking tent, we passed shelfes with cakes. Then we went to see the animals and saw sheip and calvs. We looked at lots of chickens and giese, too. My fete ached.

The best part of the day began when an announcement came over the loudspeaker: "Ladies and gentlemen, the pie-eating contest is about to begin." I rushed over to enter. They had a hundred berry pies, each cut in half. I did my best, and my tieth turned pink, but I didn't win the prize. I did, however, eat enough to have a weird nightmare last night. I dreamed about teams of clfs and mise racing to the moon on two spacecrapht. No more pie for me!

SPELLING WORDS

1. shelves
2. sheep
3. teeth
4. elves
5. mice
6. calves
7. spacecraft
8. jeans
9. feet
10. women
11. men
12. geese

1. ____Men____   7. ____geese____

2. ____women____   8. ____feet____

3. ____jeans____   9. ____teeth____

4. ____shelves____   10. ____elves____

5. ____sheep____   11. ____mice____

6. ____calves____   12. ____spacecraft____

Handwriting Tip: Bring the first upstroke of the letter *s* to a point, or it might look like an *a*. Write the Spelling Words below.

13. elves ____elves____   15. calves ____calves____

14. shelves ____shelves____   16. geese ____geese____

Harcourt

Name _____

▶ **Read the words in the picnic basket. Then write the word
that answers each riddle. Some words will be used twice.**

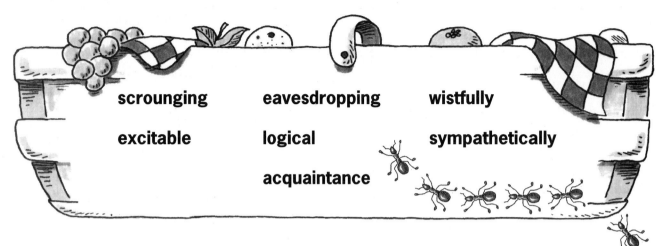

scrounging   eavesdropping   wistfully

excitable   logical   sympathetically

acquaintance

1. I look in a sad or longing way. I'm looking _____wistfully_____.

2. I overhear what you're saying. I'm _____eavesdropping_____.

3. It's easy to make me act wild. I'm _____excitable_____.

4. I search through someone's junk. I'm _____scrounging_____.

5. I think in a way that makes sense. I'm _____logical_____.

6. I'm feeling sorry for you. I'm acting _____sympathetically_____.

7. I'm getting to know you. I'm making your _____acquaintance_____.

8. I borrow things from a pile of clothes. I'm _____scrounging_____.

9. I show a lot of emotion. I'm _____excitable_____.

10. I'm listening at your keyhole. I'm _____eavesdropping_____.

Harcourt

TRY THIS! Imagine that you meet Tucker Mouse and Chester Cat. Write what you tell
them or ask them. Use at least three Vocabulary Words.

Name _____

Skill Reminder compare = tell how two things are alike
contrast = tell how they are different

▶ **Read the paragraph. Then complete the Venn diagram to show ways in which the paintings were alike and different.**
Exact wording may vary.

At the art museum Brad saw two paintings of New York City. Both were scenes of Times Square, but *Winter in the City* showed falling snow. People walking along the sidewalks were bent against the wind. It was growing dark, and a newsstand near the corner was closed. Brad liked *Summertime* better. It also showed people on the sidewalks, but the noon sun was shining brightly. The same newspaper stand was open now. The two paintings were very different, but both made Brad feel the energy of the city.

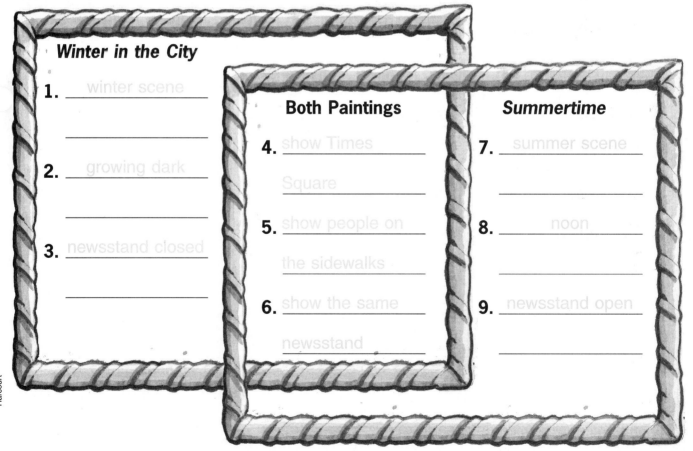

Winter in the City

1. winter scene

2. growing dark

3. newsstand closed

Both Paintings

4. show Times Square

5. show people on the sidewalks

6. show the same newsstand

Summertime

7. summer scene

8. noon

9. newsstand open

TRY THIS! Look at two of the illustrations in a story you have read. Choose two that are alike in some ways. Make a Venn diagram like the one on this page to compare and contrast the two.

Harcourt

Name _____

► As you read, start to fill in the prediction web. After you
read, write what actually happens. Possible responses are given.

Information from the Story	What I Already Know
Chester is a cricket from the country who suddenly finds himself in a big city.	Country residents sometimes find it hard to get used to city life.

Prediction

Chester will leave New York and return to Connecticut.

What Actually Happens

Chester makes friends and goes on a tour of Times Square with Tucker and Harry. Chester is fascinated by what he sees.

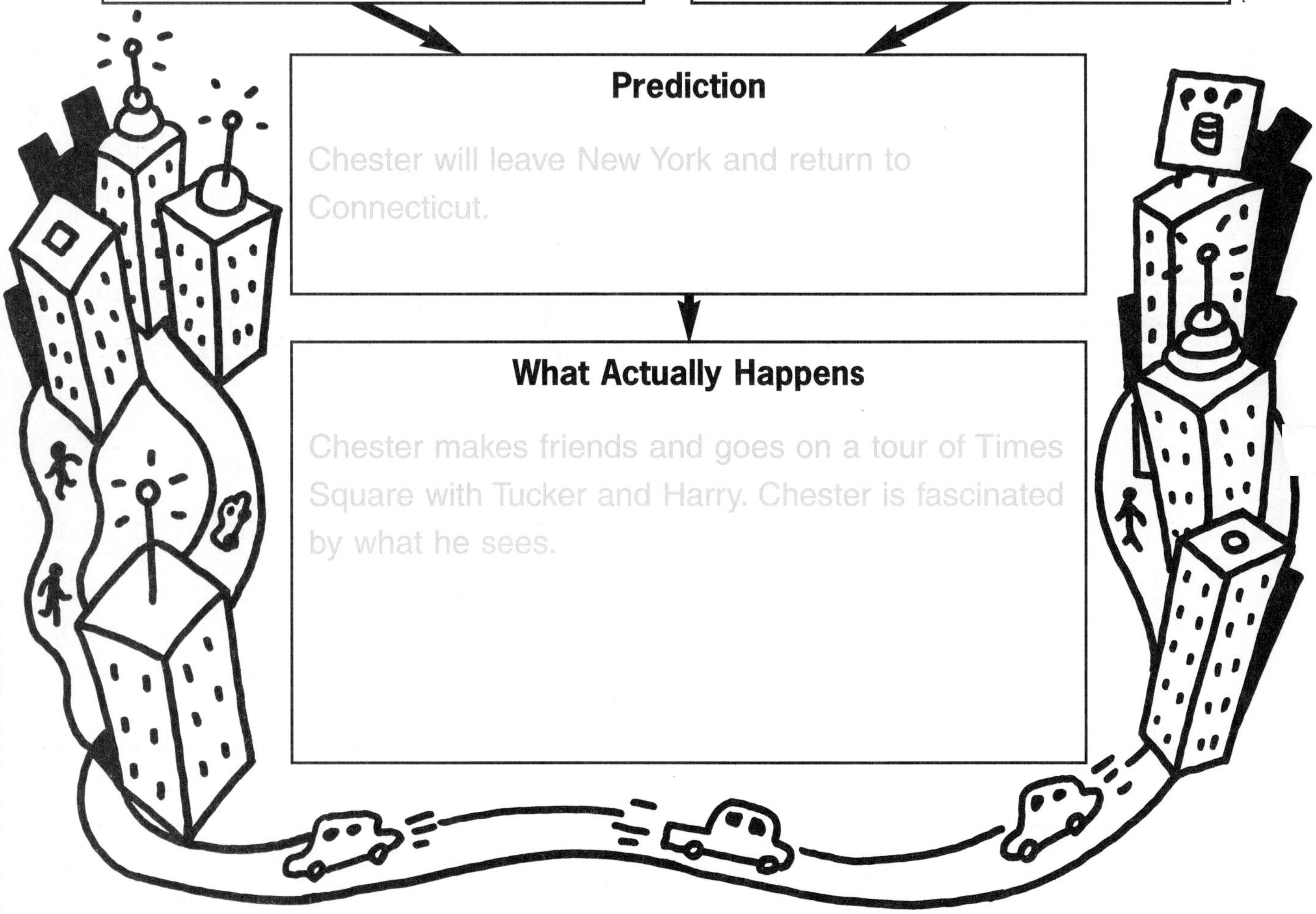

► Describe how Times Square is different from Chester's home in
Connecticut.

Possible response: Times Square is a noisy, crowded place with tall

buildings and people moving quickly. Chester's home in Connecticut is

in a tree stump, where it is quiet and peaceful.

Harcourt

Name _____

▶ **Read Susan's journal entry. Look for time-order words or
phrases that help you know the order of the events. Circle
each time-order word or phrase. Then answer the questions.**

Exact wording may vary.

I can't believe how exciting New York is! First, our plane arrived. Right after that, we took a taxi to our hotel. Then, we unpacked our suitcases and went out to explore. To begin, we just walked along Broadway. We were overwhelmed by the number of people and the number of cars. After that, we had lunch. Next, we walked east to Fifth Avenue to do some window-shopping. Then, we walked all the way to Central Park. After we got there, we bought ice cream for a snack. Later, we went back to our hotel room to rest. In the evening, we had dinner in the hotel. Finally, we went to see a Broadway musical. What a thrilling end to a wonderful day!

1. Where did Susan go just after arriving at the airport? _to the hotel_____

   _____

2. What did she do just before going out to explore? _unpacked suitcases___

   _____

3. Where did Susan walk at first? _along Broadway_____

   _____

4. Where did Susan go after window-shopping? _to Central Park_____

   _____

5. What did Susan do just before going to the theater? _had dinner_____

   _____

TRY THIS! Write about a place you might like to visit, and list a day's events.

Harcourt

▶ **Read the paragraphs. Then choose the best answer for each question. Mark the letter for that answer.**

> Ahmed's trip from Texas to New York was a long one. First, he drove to the airport in Houston. Then, he boarded a plane. The plane landed at Love Field, near downtown Dallas. Next, he took a bus to the Dallas Airport. From there he took a flight to New York.
>
> When the plane was in the air, Ahmed had lunch. Two hours later the plane landed. Finally, Ahmed reached New York.

1 First, Ahmed _____.

  A flew to Houston

  B drove to Dallas

  C drove to the Houston airport

  D took a taxi to the airport

2 Next, Ahmed _____.

  F boarded a plane

  G took a bus ride

  H flew to Dallas Airport

  J landed in New York

3 After the plane took off from Houston, _____.

  A Ahmed ate breakfast

  B the plane flew into a storm

  C the plane returned to Houston

  D the plane landed at Love Field

4 At Dallas Airport, Ahmed _____.

  F took a taxi

  G boarded a plane for New York

  H took a bus ride

  J drove back home

5 What happened next?

  A Ahmed had lunch.

  B Ahmed saw a movie.

  C Ahmed felt the plane begin to land.

  D Ahmed landed in New York.

6 What happened last?

  F Ahmed landed in Houston.

  G Ahmed arrived in New York.

  H Ahmed left Houston.

  J Ahmed landed at Dallas Airport.

Answers

1	Ⓐ Ⓑ Ⓒ Ⓓ	4	Ⓕ Ⓖ Ⓗ Ⓙ
2	Ⓕ Ⓖ Ⓗ Ⓙ	5	Ⓐ Ⓑ Ⓒ Ⓓ
3	Ⓐ Ⓑ Ⓒ Ⓓ	6	Ⓕ Ⓖ Ⓗ Ⓙ

Harcourt

▶ **Rewrite each phrase, using a possessive noun.**

1. the adventure of the hero

   the hero's adventure

2. the song of the children

   the children's song

3. the meadow belonging to the rabbits

   the rabbits' meadow

4. the story of the class

   the class's story

5. the nest of the mice

   the mice's nest

▶ **Rewrite each sentence, using the possessive form of the noun in parentheses ( ). Then write the plural possessive form of that noun.**

6. The _____ voice was strong and steady. **(cricket)**

   The cricket's voice was strong and steady. *crickets'*

   _____

7. Chester was carried to the city in the _____ picnic basket. **(family)**

   Chester was carried to the city in the family's picnic basket. *families'*

   _____

8. The _____ newsstand became his new home. **(man)**

   The man's newsstand became his new home. *men's*

   _____

TRY THIS! Write a paragraph that describes your neighborhood. Use three singular possessive nouns and two plural possessive nouns. Exchange paragraphs with a classmate to check each other's use of possessive nouns.

▶ **Complete the second phrase so that it has the same meaning as the first.**

1. the nest of a bird	a ___bird's___ nest	
2. a rider of a horse	a ___horse's___ rider	
3. the tracks of a wolf	a ___wolf's___ tracks	
4. the hats of the girls	the ___girls'___ hats	
5. the roots of two trees	two ___trees'___ roots	
6. a friend of his parents	his ___parents'___ friend	
7. the idea of the students	the ___students'___ idea	
8. the athletes of the class	the ___class's___ athletes	

SPELLING WORDS

1. team's
2. players'
3. bird's
4. wolf's
5. horse's
6. class's
7. group's
8. girls'
9. students'
10. trees'
11. parents'
12. owners'

▶ **Write the correct Spelling Word.**

9. of the team ___team's___

10. of the group ___group's___

11. of the owners ___owners'___

12. of the players ___players'___

Handwriting Tip: Use equal spacing between letters. Leave one pencil-width between words. Write the Spelling Words below.

the wolf's den

13. players' ___players'___   15. students' ___students'___

14. horse's ___horse's___   16. class's ___class's___

▶ **Write a word from the box to complete each sentence.**

| tundra | ceases | bonding | piteously | surrender | abundant |

1. The _____tundra_____ is so cold and empty!

4. No matter what happens, do not _____surrender_____ to the cold. You must return with food.

2. Be brave. Stop howling so _____piteously_____!

5. Our pups are _____bonding_____ as they play together.

3. I'll go hunting so we'll have _____abundant_____ food.

6. For those pups, the fun never _____ceases_____!

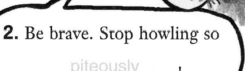

▶ **Write the word from the box above that means the *opposite* of each word.**

7. scarce _____abundant_____   **9.** victory _____surrender_____

8. begins _____ceases_____   **10.** proudly _____piteously_____

TRY THIS! Choose an animal you would like to be. Describe your day as that animal, using at least two Vocabulary Words.

Harcourt

Name _____

Skill Reminder   **Look for time-order words to give you clues about the order in which events happen.**

▶ **Read the paragraph. Then complete each sentence to tell the order of the events.** Exact wording may vary.

Crocodiles may look fierce, but they take good care of their young. The female crocodile begins her mothering by burying her eggs in a soft, sandy riverbank. Next, she guards them for three months so other animals won't bother them. When it's time for the eggs to hatch, the babies call to the mother. She hears their calls and uncovers the eggs. Then, she breaks the shells with her mouth. After all the eggs have hatched, the mother carries the babies in her mouth to shallow water. Then, she lets the babies go. They will live in this safe place for several weeks with their mother nearby. Finally, they will be able to take care of themselves. They will live up to seventy years.

The first thing a mother crocodile does to care for her eggs is

to **(1)** _____ bury them in a riverbank _____ . Next, she

(2) _____ guards them for three months _____ . She uncovers

the eggs when **(3)** _____ the babies call _____ , and she

(4) _____ breaks the shells _____ . As soon as all the eggs

have hatched, she **(5)** _____ carries the babies to shallow water _____ . After

they reach the water, she **(6)** _____ lets the babies go _____ .

For several weeks the babies will **(7)** _____ live in this safe place _____ .

Finally, the baby crocodiles **(8)** _____ will be able to take care of themselves _____ .

SCHOOL-HOME CONNECTION With your child, talk about a special celebration in your family or community. Help your child use time-order words to list the order in which the events took place.

Harcourt

Name _____

▶ **Fill in the first two columns of the K-W-L chart. Then use information from the story to fill in the last column.**

Possible responses are given.

K	W	L
What I Know	**What I Want to Know**	**What I Learned**
Wolves live in a pack.	How do wolves find their place in the pack?	Some are leaders. Some are hunters. The pups fight and find their places.
Wolves grow quickly.	How do wolves care for their young?	The mother gives milk for 7 weeks. After 4 weeks, the yearling baby-sits. The father coughs up food for the pups to eat.
Wolves eat meat.	How do wolf pups learn to survive?	They hunt by sniffing for the scent of an injured animal.

▶ **Write a brief description of how wolf pups change during their first year.**

Possible response: They start out as tiny, helpless creatures with no sense

of smell. After a year, they are full-grown animals that can pick up scents

easily and hunt large animals successfully.

Name _____

▶ Read the paragraphs and the questions on this page and
the next page. Then use the QAR (Question-Answer Relationship)
strategy. Write a strategy from the box to answer each question.
Exact wording may vary.

| **Right There** | **Think and Search** | **On My Own** |
| (in text) | (inferred from text) | (prior knowledge or research) |

Can you guess what animal can travel the length of a minivan in just one hop? It's
the kangaroo. Kangaroos, which are marsupials, use their strong tails for balance
when they hop. When they land, their tails help prop them up. Kangaroos usually
move about by taking smaller leaps. The average jump is about six feet. Kangaroos
can crawl, too. When they are grazing, they crawl awkwardly on all four feet.

In what two ways can kangaroos move about?

1. Strategy: Right There _____

2. Answer: Kangaroos jump and crawl. _____

_____

Why would it be hard for a kangaroo to jump if it
didn't have a tail?

3. Strategy: Think and Search _____

4. Answer: It needs its tail for balance. _____

_____

What is a marsupial?

5. Strategy: On My Own _____

6. Answer: A marsupial is an animal that _____

carries its young in a pouch. _____

Harcourt

GO ON

A baby kangaroo is called a joey. When a joey is born, it still can't survive outside the mother's pouch. It isn't much bigger than your thumbnail. It has no hair and can't see, but its front legs are already strong. Soon after birth it begins crawling toward the mother's pouch. The joey makes the six-inch trip to the pouch in about three minutes. When it reaches the pouch, it begins feeding on milk. The pouch will be the joey's home for the next six months.

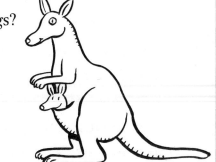

Why does a new-born joey need to have strong front legs?

1. Strategy: _Think and Search_____

2. Answer: _It needs strong front legs_____

_so it can crawl into its mother's pouch._____

Kangaroos come in many different sizes. The red kangaroo may grow to six feet tall, but the musky rat kangaroo is only about the size of a rabbit. In between are the wallaroos and the smaller wallabies. There are more than 45 different types of kangaroos.

Which kind of kangaroo is the smallest?

3. Strategy: _Right There_____

4. Answer: _the musky rat kangaroo_____

_____

What are wallaroos like?

5. Strategy: _On My Own_____

6. Answer: _Possible response: Wallaroos are one of the larger species_

of kangaroos called great kangaroos. They live only in Australia in the

_wild on dry, rocky hills._____

TRY THIS! Think of an animal you know something about. Write as many questions as you can about that animal. Make a list of places a person might look to find the answers.

Harcourt

Name _____

▶ Use one or more test-taking strategies in the box to answer each question from the choices below. Then write the letters of the strategies you used to answer the question.

A. Find and use key words.	**C. Check back to the paragraph.**
B. Eliminate wrong or silly answers.	**D. Use signal word *who* or *where*.**

    Imagine living part of your life in the water and part on land! That's what seals, sea lions, and walruses do. They are *pinnipeds*, which means "fin-footed." Pinnipeds are skillful and graceful swimmers, but they look awkward as they waddle along on land, using their flippers as feet. In the sea, they must come to the surface to breathe, since they are mammals, who breathe air.

Where do seals, sea lions, and walruses live?

   1. Answer: _both on land and in water_____

     on land   **both on land and in water**   **in the air**

   2. Strategies used: _(Answers may vary.) A, C, D_____

What does the word *pinniped* mean?

   3. Answer: _fin-footed_____

     seal   **without fins**   **fin-footed**

   4. Strategies used: _(Answers may vary.) A, C_____

Why do pinnipeds walk awkwardly?

   5. Answer: _They use flippers._____

     They can't swim.   **They use flippers.**   **They are fish.**

   6. Strategies used: _(Answers may vary.) A, B, C_____

Why can't pinnipeds breathe under water?

   7. Answer: _They are mammals._____

     They are mammals.   **They don't have noses.**   **They waddle.**

   8. Strategies used: _(Answers may vary.) A, B, C_____

Harcourt

Name _____

▶ **Rewrite each item, using abbreviations.**

1. 22 ounces _____ 22 oz. _____

2. Mister Stephen Washburn _____ Mr. Stephen Washburn _____

3. 35 miles, 25 feet _____ 35 mi., 25 ft. _____

4. 62 Central Avenue _____ 62 Central Ave. _____

5. 6.4 kilometers _____ 6.4 km _____

6. Friday, February 25 _____ Fri., Feb. 25 _____

▶ **Circle the correct abbreviation for each item.**

7. Snowy Boulevard	(Snowy Blvd.)	*OR*	Snowy Bd.
8. 30 centimeters	(30 cm)	*OR*	30 cms.
9. Tuesday, April 12	T'day., Ap. 12	*OR*	(Tues., Apr. 12)
10. 5 hours	5 hrs	*OR*	(5 hr)

TRY THIS! Write a story about a trip you would like to take. Use words that can be abbreviated. Share your story in a small group. See if your classmates can abbreviate your words correctly.

Harcourt

Name _____

▶ **Write the abbreviation for the underlined word.**

1. I was born in <u>September</u>.   _____Sept._____

2. Dad saw the pups on <u>Friday</u>.   _____Fri._____

3. On <u>Saturday</u> we saw a movie.   _____Sat._____

4. We got a puppy in <u>December</u>.   _____Dec._____

5. That pup weighs over a <u>pound</u>.   _____lb._____

6. Pups are fed from a <u>teaspoon</u>.   _____tsp._____

SPELLING WORDS
1. Pres.
2. Dr.
3. Ave.
4. Hwy.
5. Rd.
6. St.
7. Fri.
8. Sat.
9. Sept.
10. Dec.
11. tsp.
12. lb.

▶ **Write the abbreviation of the word in parentheses.**

7. Coast _____Hwy._____ **(Highway)**

8. _____Dr._____ Kwan **(Doctor)**

9. First _____St._____ **(Street)**

10. _____Pres._____ Taft **(President)**

11. 160 Bird _____Ave._____ **(Avenue)**

12. 835 Rossi _____Rd._____ **(Road)**

Handwriting Tip: When you write a capital letter, be sure it reaches the top writing line. Write the Spelling Words below. $\mathcal{P}$

13. St. _____St._____   **15.** Dec. _____Dec._____

14. Ave. _____Ave._____   **16.** Pres. _____Pres._____

SCHOOL-HOME CONNECTION With your child, send letters to family members or friends whose addresses are different. Help your child write the envelopes using the correct abbreviations.

Harcourt

Name _____

▶ Read the words below. Then read the words in groups on each cactus. Write the word that belongs in each group.

| brush | spiny | teeming | habitat | topple | decomposes |

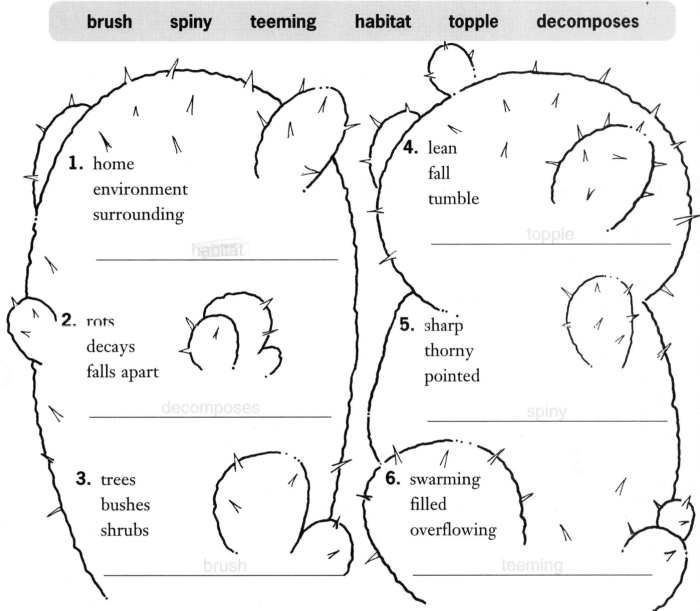

1. home
   environment
   surrounding

   _____ habitat

2. rots
   decays
   falls apart

   _____ decomposes

3. trees
   bushes
   shrubs

   _____ brush

4. lean
   fall
   tumble

   _____ topple

5. sharp
   thorny
   pointed

   _____ spiny

6. swarming
   filled
   overflowing

   _____ teeming

▶ Write a Vocabulary Word to complete each analogy.

7. *Tree* is to *forest* as *bush* is to _____ brush .

8. *Rain* is to *rainy* as *spine* is to _____ spiny .

9. *Goes* is to *stops* as *grows* is to _____ decomposes .

10. *Film* is to *movie* as *home* is to _____ habitat .

SCHOOL-HOME CONNECTION With your child, talk about plants, flowers, and trees that grow nearby. Describe how they look, using at least two Vocabulary Words.

Touch a Dream **105**

Harcourt

Name _____

▶ Fill in the first two columns of the K-W-L chart. Then use
information from the story to fill in the last column. Possible responses are
given.

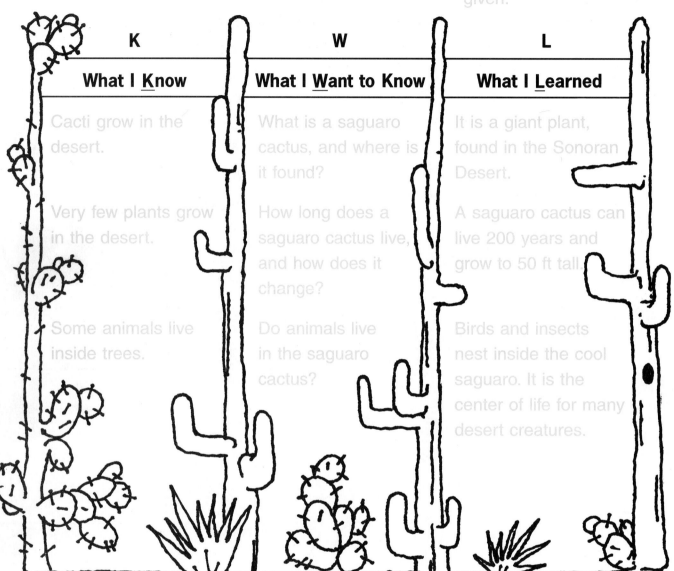

K	W	L
What I Know	**What I Want to Know**	**What I Learned**
Cacti grow in the desert.	What is a saguaro cactus, and where is it found?	It is a giant plant, found in the Sonoran Desert.
Very few plants grow in the desert.	How long does a saguaro cactus live, and how does it change?	A saguaro cactus can live 200 years and grow to 50 ft tall.
Some animals live inside trees.	Do animals live in the saguaro cactus?	Birds and insects nest inside the cool saguaro. It is the center of life for many desert creatures.

▶ List five ways in which the saguaro cactus helps desert animals.
Possible responses are given.

1. Elf owls and woodpeckers make their homes in it. _____

2. Insects and birds eat the sweet, juicy pulp of its fruit. _____

3. Birds, bats, and insects drink the nectar of its flowers. _____

4. Lizards and spiders eat insects found in the cactus. _____

5. Scorpions and rattlesnakes live in dead saguaros. _____

Harcourt

Name _____

▶ **Read the paragraph. Then answer the questions.**

    Deserts do not have to be hot. They only have to be dry. Any area of land that gets ten inches or less of precipitation in a year is classified as a desert. Some deserts are very cold. Two of these cold deserts are at the North Pole and South Pole. Parts of the polar regions have a lot of water, but it is frozen all year long. Frozen water is not much help to plants and animals. Some of the Antarctic region is so cold and so high up that there is very little precipitation. *Precipitation* is any form of water that falls to earth. Rain, snow, sleet, and hail are kinds of precipitation.

1. This paragraph is an example of _____ expository nonfiction _____.
   a. fiction
   b. expository nonfiction
   c. persuasive nonfiction

2. What is the main purpose of the paragraph? (Exact wording may vary.)
   to give information about cold deserts

3. Is the paragraph organized by main idea and details or by sequence of events?
   main idea and details

4. What is the main idea? Some deserts are very cold.

5. Which of these details supports the main idea? Parts of the polar
   regions have a lot of water, but it is frozen all year long.
   a. Some deserts are very hot.
   b. Parts of the polar regions have a lot of water, but it is frozen all year long.
   c. Some polar regions have precipitation.

▶ **Choose from the words or phrases below each line to
complete each sentence. Write the answer on the line.**

The South American desert toad has adapted to life in the desert in an unusual
way. When there is a rain shower in the summer, the toad absorbs moisture through
its skin. Then it burrows into the mud. There it becomes inactive. Its heart rate slows
down, and the animal is very still for months at a time. When rains come again, the

toad comes out of its underground home to find food.
The female toad lays her eggs in a pool of rainwater.
The baby toads hatch and develop. When the pool
dries up, the babies burrow into the mud to wait
for the rains to come again, just as their parents
had done.

South American desert toad

Readers can tell that this paragraph is expository nonfiction because it gives

(1) _____ information _____ about the desert toad but does not
    stories   information   directions

(2) _____ tell a story _____ .
    tell a story   give facts   give instructions

The main purpose of this paragraph is to

(3) _____ give information _____ .
    give the author's opinion   persuade readers   give information

One clue that this paragraph is expository nonfiction is that it has a

(4) _____ picture and caption _____ along with it.
    heading   diagram   picture and caption

The paragraph is organized by

(5) _____ sequence of events _____ .
    main idea and details   sequence of events   giving directions

**TRY
THIS!** Find a feature in a science textbook. List the clues that tell you if the
feature is an example of expository nonfiction. Write whether it is organized
according to main idea and details or sequence of events.

Harcourt

Name _____

▶ **Use the definitions in the Desert Dictionary to help you write labels for the saguaro cactus drawing.**

Desert Dictionary

boot   a hard wall that forms around holes in a cactus skin

flower   the part of a plant that has colorful petals and makes the plant's seeds

javelina   a desert hog that eats cactus roots

pleat   long fold on the skin of a cactus

pollen   a yellowish powder that fertilizes a plant

pulp   the soft, juicy part of a plant or fruit

seedling   young plant grown from seeds

spine   sharp, pointed growth on a plant

Fruit

1. _____spine_____

2. _____flower_____

3. _____pulp_____

4. _____pollen_____

5. _____boot_____

6. _____pleat_____

7. _____seedling_____

8. _____javelina_____

Harcourt

Name _____

▶ **Underline the pronouns in these sentences. If a pronoun has an antecedent in the same sentence, draw an arrow from the pronoun to the antecedent.**

1. Darryl jumped when he saw a wolf spider.

2. Rita said, "I don't like spiders much, either."

3. Darryl saw a praying mantis and a lizard watching it.

4. Rita called to Darryl and showed him a hawk flying overhead.

5. Some birds hunt for lizards and eat them.

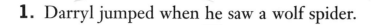

▶ **Rewrite these sentences, replacing the underlined words with pronouns.**

6. Rob walked up to the saguaro and took a close look at the saguaro. Rob

   walked up to the saguaro and took a close look at it.

   _____

7. "Marsha, come here," Rob called. "Marsha should see what Rob found."

   "Marsha, come here," Rob called. "You should see what I found."

   _____

8. "The inside of that hole is hard. Maybe the hole was a nest." The inside

   of that hole is hard. Maybe it was a nest."

9. "The hole might have given a mother elf owl and her babies a home." The

   hole might have given them a home."

   _____

10. Marsha replied, "Rob, maybe Rob and Marsha should call Ellie. Ellie would

    like to see this." Marsha replied, "Rob, maybe we should call Ellie. She

    would like to see this."

SCHOOL-HOME CONNECTION With your child, list the names of ten people that everyone in your family knows. Ask your child to write five pairs of sentences using a name in one sentence and a pronoun to replace it in the other sentence.

Harcourt

Name _____

▶ The letters of the underlined words are mixed up. Write the correct Spelling Words on the lines.

SPELLING WORDS

1. *weight*
2. *ceiling*
3. *field*
4. *reindeer*
5. *freight*
6. *eighteen*
7. *neighbor*
8. *receive*
9. *weird*
10. *chief*
11. *believe*
12. *piece*

1. This cactus looks <u>drewi</u>. _____ weird

2. I <u>libeeev</u> it's true. _____ believe

3. I think the giant cactus is "<u>fceih</u>" among the desert plants. _____ chief

4. Guess the <u>thewig</u> of this plant. _____ weight

5. A <u>ecipe</u> of this cactus died. _____ piece

6. We heard a <u>trgeifh</u> train. _____ freight

7. Our <u>bgeniroh</u> has a cactus. _____ neighbor

8. He'll <u>cireeve</u> a new plant. _____ receive

▶ Write the Spelling Word that names each picture.

9. _____ reindeer

11. _____ ceiling

10. _____ eighteen

12. _____ field

Handwriting Tip: When you write the letter combination *ei* or *ie*, loop the *e* and not the *i*. Write the Spelling Words below. *ei*

13. weight _____ weight

15. weird _____ weird

14. field _____ field

16. piece _____ piece

Harcourt

Name _____

▶ **Write the word from the box that matches each clue below.
The message in the shaded area of the answers tells you
another name for an inventor.**

document	prosthetic	device	disabilities
circular	scholarship	modify	

1. something made for
   a special use
   d e v i c e

2. round
   c i r c u l a r

3. an official paper or record
   d o c u m e n t

4. injuries or problems
   d i s a b i l i t i e s

5. artificial (body part)
   p r o s t h e t i c

6. to change
   m o d i f y

7. a student's knowledge
   s c h o l a r s h i p

▶ **Write the word from the box above that is related to each word below.**

8. circle _____circular_____

9. unable _____disabilities_____

10. school _____scholarship_____

TRY THIS! Briefly describe an invention you think would help others. Use some
Vocabulary Words.

Harcourt

Name _____

▶ **Before you read, complete the first two columns of the
SQ3R chart. Complete the third column during and after
reading.** Possible responses are given.

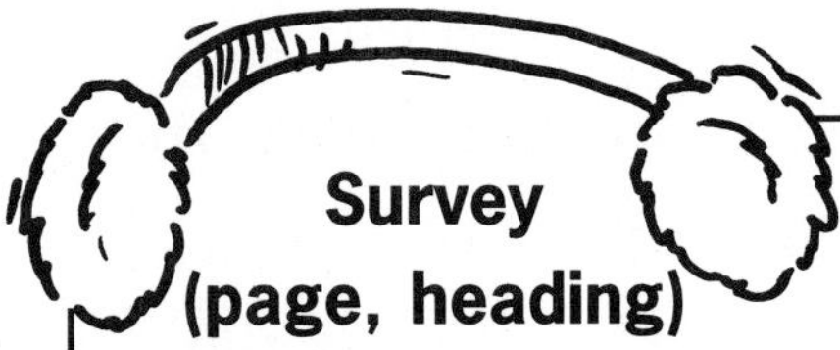

Survey (page, heading)	Question	Read, Recite, Review (answer)
page 348 Kids Are Inventors, Too	What did Chester Greenwood invent?	earmuffs
page 350 The Prosthetic Catch & Throw Device	What is a prosthetic catch & throw device?	a glove that allows someone with no arm to catch and throw a ball
page 352 The All-in-One Washer/Dryer	How does an all-in-one washer/dryer work?	Clothes from the washer drop into the dryer automatically without having to be removed first.
page 354 The Conserve Sprinkler	What does a conserve sprinkler do?	It saves water when sprinkling trees and shrubs.

▶ **Write a one-sentence summary of the whole selection.**

Possible response: By using their imagination, kids are able to

invent items that are highly useful and easy to use.

Harcourt

Name _____

▶ **Read each paragraph. Then write the answers on the lines.**
Exact wording may vary.

Yo-yos are popular as toys and as items to collect, too. People in the United States have been playing with yo-yos since about 1929. Over the years children and adults have learned to do yo-yo tricks. Collectors often pay money for old wooden yo-yos or collect special models that whistle or glow in the dark.

1. What is the main idea? Yo-yos are popular as toys and as items to

collect, too.

List three supporting details.

2. People in the United States have been playing with yo-yos since about 1929.

3. Over the years children and adults have learned to do yo-yo tricks.

4. Collectors often pay money for old yo-yos or special models.

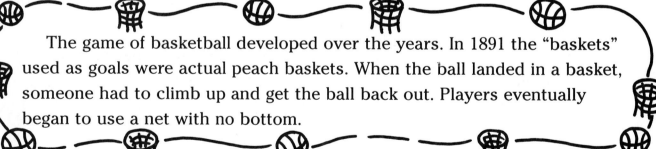

The game of basketball developed over the years. In 1891 the "baskets" used as goals were actual peach baskets. When the ball landed in a basket, someone had to climb up and get the ball back out. Players eventually began to use a net with no bottom.

5. What is the main idea? Basketball developed over a period of time.

List two supporting details.

6. At first the balls were shot at peach baskets.

7. Players began using nets with no bottoms.

 TRY THIS! Plan a paragraph explaining what you know about a toy or game you like. Write the main idea. Then list three or four supporting details for the main idea.

Harcourt

Name _____

▶ **Read the paragraphs. Then read each question, and decide which is the best answer. Mark the letter for that answer.**

Dude ranching began more than a hundred years ago. Visitors from the East wanted to experience ranch life, so they went west and paid to stay on a ranch. The ranch hands called these visitors "dudes." In 1904 the Eaton family charged dudes $10 a week to stay and work on their ranch.

Today dude ranches are popular vacation spots for families, but guests don't do farm work! They can ride horseback or raft down a river. They may learn to twirl a rope or may take square-dancing lessons. Dude ranching is a way for ranchers to make extra money and for visitors to have fun.

1 Which sentence from the passage tells the main idea?

(A) Dude ranching began more than a hundred years ago.

(B) The ranch hands called these visitors "dudes."

(C) Dude ranching is a way for ranchers to make extra money and for visitors to have fun.

(D) They can ride horseback or raft down a river.

2 Which of these details supports the main idea?

(F) Dude ranching began more than a hundred years ago.

(G) Dude ranches are popular vacation spots for families.

(H) Guests don't know much about ranching.

(J) Guests must learn to ride horses.

3 Which of these details supports the main idea?

(A) Ranch hands called the visitors "dudes."

(B) Ranch hands taught dudes to round up cattle.

(C) Nobody had a dude ranch before 1882.

(D) Visitors would pay to stay on a ranch.

4 Which detail *does not* support the main idea?

(F) Ranchers charge visitors to come and stay.

(G) Dude ranching is still popular.

(H) Families have fun at dude ranches.

(J) Everybody likes river rafting.

Harcourt

Name _____

▶ **Read the directions for making a yarn animal. Then answer the questions.**

Materials:

 drawing paper

pencil

waxed paper

4 paper clips

 1/2 cup classroom glue

1/4 cup water

small foil pan or other container you can throw away

 thick yarn

Directions:

Draw the outline of an animal so that every line touches another line.

Cover the drawing paper with waxed paper. Clip the two sheets together.

Mix glue and water in a disposable container.

Cut a piece of yarn and soak it in the glue. Lift the yarn and squeeze so it won't drip.

Lay the strip of yarn along the drawn outline.

Cut and soak other pieces of yarn, and add them to the design. Overlap the strips so they will stick together.

Let the yarn design dry overnight. Then remove it from the waxed paper.

1. Which should you do first, cut the yarn or soak it in glue?

Cut the yarn.

2. What should you do with the soaked yarn before you put it on the drawing?

Squeeze it a little so it won't drip.

3. What may happen if you do not overlap the strips of yarn?

(Exact wording may vary.) The strips of yarn may not stick together.

4. How long should you let your yarn animal dry? overnight

5. What is the last step? Remove the yarn design from the waxed paper.

6. What might happen if you do not follow the directions in order?

(Exact wording may vary.) The yarn animal might not turn out right.

 SCHOOL-HOME CONNECTION Ask your child to write directions for playing a game that two people can play. Then follow the directions to play the game together.

Harcourt

Name _____

▶ **Rewrite each sentence, replacing the underlined word or words with a pronoun. Write *subject* or *object* to identify each pronoun you use.**

1. <u>Chester</u> made earmuffs for everyone. He made earmuffs for everyone. subject

2. Mr. Parsons told Josh about <u>David Potter</u>. Mr. Parsons told Josh about him. object

3. <u>Josh and David</u> worked together to design a glove. They worked together to design a glove. subject

4. Soon David played for <u>the Spring Branch Mustangs</u>. Soon David played for them. object

5. <u>Reeba Daniel</u> invented a washer/dryer. She invented a washer/dryer. subject

6. <u>Reba's invention</u> won a prize. It won a prize. subject

▶ **Rewrite each sentence. Correct any errors in the use of pronouns.**

7. Josh and me helped David. Josh and I helped David. (OR We helped David.)

8. David thanked me and Josh for helping. David thanked Josh and me for helping. (OR David thanked us for helping.)

TRY THIS! Write three separate sentences about an invention that you find useful. Then put your sentences together in a paragraph, using pronouns to replace nouns as needed.

Harcourt

Name _____

▶ **Write a Spelling Word to complete each sentence.**

1. Earn _____money_____ with your own invention.

2. Invent a special knife to carve a_____turkey_____.

3. The knives we _____already_____ have are good.

4. Invent a new _____hockey_____ stick.

5. Invent a machine to make a snack whenever you

   feel _____hungry_____.

6. Invent a flying bike that goes from the

   _____valley_____ up to the mountaintop.

7. Invent a robot that moves like a _____monkey_____.

▶ **Write the Spelling Word that best means the
opposite of each word or phrase.**

8. light   _____heavy_____

9. late   _____early_____

10. everybody   _____nobody_____

11. not one   _____every_____

12. huge   _____tiny_____

SPELLING WORDS
1. tiny
2. hockey
3. heavy
4. every
5. money
6. turkey
7. early
8. hungry
9. already
10. valley
11. nobody
12. monkey

Handwriting Tip: Do not close the top of the
letter *y*, or it might look like *g*. Write the Spelling
Words below.

tiny

13. tiny _____tiny_____   15. hockey _____hockey_____

14. heavy _____heavy_____   16. monkey _____monkey_____

Harcourt

Name _____

▶ **Write the word from the box that matches each clue.**

muttered	strengthening	sculptor
straightaway	retorted	alibi

1. giving more energy to

2. one who makes statues

3. talked in a low voice

4. answered back

5. an excuse given by one accused

6. immediately

2. sculptor
3. muttered
1. strengthening
4. retorted
5. alibi
6. straightaway

▶ **Write the word from the box above that means the *opposite* of each word.**

7. asked _____ retorted

8. weakening _____ strengthening

9. shouted _____ muttered

10. later _____ straightaway

TRY THIS! Describe a time when you looked for something you lost. Tell what happened, using some Vocabulary Words.

Harcourt

Name _____

| Skill Reminder | main idea = central idea of the passage |
| | details = information about the main idea |

▶ **Read the paragraphs. Then answer the questions.**
Exact wording may vary.

When Abraham Lincoln was a boy, schools on the Kentucky frontier were very basic. Anyone who could read, write, and do simple arithmetic could be a teacher. There were few books, and paper was scarce. Often the students made their own arithmetic books. Children of different ages went to school in the same room.

1. What is the main idea? When Abraham Lincoln was a boy, schools on the Kentucky frontier were very basic.

List three supporting details from the paragraph:

2. Anyone who could read, write, and do simple arithmetic could be a teacher.

3. There were few books, and paper was scarce.

4. Children of different ages went to school in the same room.

Many children on the frontier had to walk long distances to school. School buildings often were not well heated. At home, the children studied by candlelight or by the light of the fireplace.

5. What is the main idea? Children on the frontier had to overcome difficulties to get an education.

6. Is the main idea stated in the paragraph? no

List two supporting details from the paragraph:

7. Many children had to walk long distances to school.

8. School buildings were cold in winter.

SCHOOL-HOME CONNECTION With your child, discuss a book he or she enjoyed reading. Ask your child to tell the main idea of the book and give some important details.

Harcourt

Name _____

▶ **Complete the character map below. Write important
information about each of the characters.** Possible
responses are given.

Encyclopedia Brown

is a detective.

does not jump to conclusions.

asks few questions and listens
carefully.

proves that Desmoana is the thief.

Pablo

sculpts a nose that is stolen.

brags about his sculpture.

is quick to accuse Desmoana
without proof.

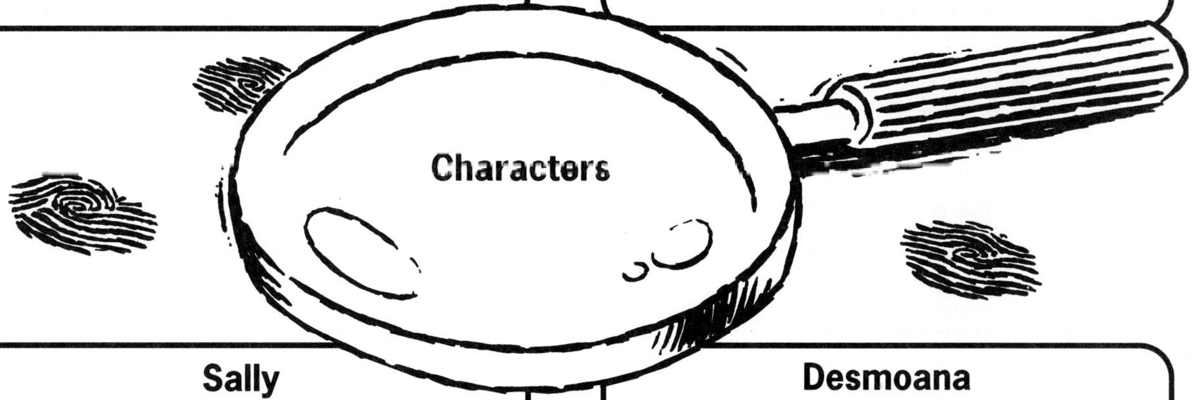

Characters

Sally

helps Encyclopedia Brown.

asks good questions.

figures out important things quickly.

Desmoana

denies stealing the nose.

brags about her bike-riding
abilities.

is proven to be the thief.

▶ **Write a one-sentence summary explaining how Encyclopedia Brown
figures out that Desmoana is the thief.**

Possible response: She claims she hasn't ridden her purple bicycle for a

year, yet she does bicycle tricks without hesitation, proving she's lying.

Harcourt

Name _____

▶ **On the lines, write the answers to the questions.**
Exact wording may vary.

Beginning: Matt's mother, Mrs. Stevens, complains that paper clips are disappearing from her desk at home. Both Matt and his father say they haven't been borrowing any of them. Matt remembers that his pet bird, Pete, likes shiny things.

1. What is the problem in the story? Mrs. Stevens's paper clips have been disappearing from her desk at home.

2. What other information does Mrs. Stevens need to solve the problem?
She needs to find out if Pete has been out of his cage at the times the paper clips have disappeared.

Middle: Matt says he has been leaving Pete's cage door open when he leaves for school. Mrs. Stevens says she has noticed that the paper clips have disappeared during school hours. They look in Pete's cage and find a dime and a plastic ring, but no paper clips. Mr. Stevens says he has noticed that Pete often perches on a shelf above the fireplace.

3. What might the Stevens family do next to solve the problem? They might look on the shelf where Pete often perches.

4. What makes you think that? The paper clips aren't in the birdcage, so Pete may be hiding them somewhere else.

Ending: Matt feels along the shelf but finds nothing. Then his hand bumps against a jar on the shelf. The jar falls, spilling paper clips onto the floor. Pete swoops down, chirping happily, and picks up a clip with his beak.

5. How is the problem solved? Matt knocks over a jar and discovers where Pete has been hiding the paper clips.

Harcourt

TRY THIS! Write a beginning for a mystery story. Be sure to state the problem. Then list ways the characters might solve the problem.

Name _____

The Case of
Pablo's Nose

Extending
Vocabulary:
Multiple-Meaning
Words

▶ **Write the correct meaning of each underlined word.
Choose from the meanings in the box.**

> **ground:** a. the part of the earth that is solid b. crushed into small pieces
> **nose:** a. the part of the face used for breathing b. to push forward gently
> **snapped:** a. broke suddenly b. spoke sharply
> **started:** a. began b. moved suddenly from surprise
> **store:** a. a place to shop b. to keep things in a place for future use
> **windows:** a. a computer term b. clear parts of a building, made of glass

1. Desmoana <u>started</u> when Encyclopedia accused her of lying.

Started means "moved suddenly from surprise."

2. The <u>ground</u> was covered with snow when the
children woke up in the morning.

Ground means "the part of the earth that is solid."

3. A twig <u>snapped</u> under Encyclopedia's feet as he crept through the woods.

Snapped means "broke suddenly."

4. Encyclopedia <u>started</u> the day with a good breakfast.

Started means "began."

5. Encyclopedia used separate <u>windows</u> on his computer screen to divide the
information he needed to <u>store</u>.

Windows is a computer term

and *store* means "to keep things in a place for future use."

6. Encyclopedia's dog began to <u>nose</u> the door open.

Nose means "to push forward gently."

7. The suspect <u>snapped</u> at the detective when he asked her a tough question.

Snapped means "spoke sharply."

8. Pablo <u>ground</u> plaster and water into a paste before beginning his art project.

Ground means "crushed into small pieces."

Name _____

▶ **Write the possessive pronouns that could replace each group of words below.**

	Before a Noun	Not Before a Noun
1. Martha Katz's	her	hers
2. the townspeople's	their	theirs
3. belonging to me	my	mine
4. Pablo's	his	his
5. owned by Sally and me	our	ours

▶ **Rewrite each sentence, replacing the underlined words with possessive pronouns.**

6. Pablo did not ride <u>Pablo's</u> bike to Encyclopedia's house.

   Pablo did not ride his bike to Encyclopedia's house.

7. Pablo and Sally had almost made up <u>Pablo's and Sally's</u> minds.

   Pablo and Sally had almost made up their minds.

8. Sally eagerly gave Encyclopedia <u>Sally's</u> opinion.

   Sally eagerly gave Encyclopedia her opinion.

9. "Yes, that bike is <u>Desmoana's</u>," admitted Desmoana at last.

   "Yes, that bike is mine," admitted Desmoana at last.

10. "You and I make a great team, Sally," Encyclopedia said. "The credit for solving this case is <u>Sally's and Encyclopedia's</u>."

    "You and I make a great team, Sally," Encyclopedia said. "The credit

    for solving this case is ours."

TRY THIS! What are some of your favorite things? Use possessive pronouns to write five sentences about the items. Include examples of both kinds of possessive pronouns.

Harcourt

▶ **Read each word. Then write a Spelling Word with the opposite meaning by adding the prefix *un-* or *dis-*.**

1. clean _____unclean_____

2. like _____dislike_____

3. happy _____unhappy_____

4. used _____unused_____

5. kind _____unkind_____

6. friendly _____unfriendly_____

7. heard _____unheard_____

8. agree _____disagree_____

SPELLING WORDS
1. *unused*
2. *dislike*
3. *unclean*
4. *unheard*
5. *disagree*
6. *disabled*
7. *unkind*
8. *unfriendly*
9. *unable*
10. *unhappy*
11. *unsafe*
12. *disobey*

▶ **Write a Spelling Word to complete each sentence.**

9. This intersection is _____unsafe_____.

10. Too many drivers _____disobey_____ the stop sign.

11. People who use wheelchairs are

_____unable_____ to cross the street here.

12. There are no curb ramps for people

who are _____disabled_____.

Handwriting Tip: Take care to hold your pen or pencil properly—about an inch from the point, between the thumb and first finger. Write the Spelling Words below.

13. unkind _____unkind_____   **15.** unhappy _____unhappy_____

14. unable _____unable_____   **16.** unsafe _____unsafe_____

► Choose a word from the bricks to complete each sentence
below. Fill in one letter per blank. Some words are used twice.

| thrifty | generous | roguish | rascally | fascinated |

"Notice for House Guests."

1. We serve g e n e r o u s portions, so eat all you like.

2. We try to be t h r i f t y, so please do not waste food.

3. If you are f a s c i n a t e d by something you see here,
   please ask about it.

4. The r a s c a l l y activity of stealing towels is illegal.

5. R o g u i s h house guests may not return here.

6. We charge very little, so please be a t h r i f t y guest.

7. Feel free to leave a g e n e r o u s tip at the end of your stay.

8. We are f a s c i n a t e d by interesting stories, so please
   share any you may have!

► Fill in the blanks below.

9. Write two Vocabulary Words that are synonyms.

   _____roguish_____   _____rascally_____

10. Write two Vocabulary Words that are antonyms.

   _____thrifty_____   _____generous_____

TRY THIS! Make a list of rules you think parents should follow, using at least two
Vocabulary Words.

Harcourt

Name _____

▶ **Complete the Venn diagram below by telling how the old
woman is different from the two young men. Then tell
how all three characters are the same.** Possible responses are given.

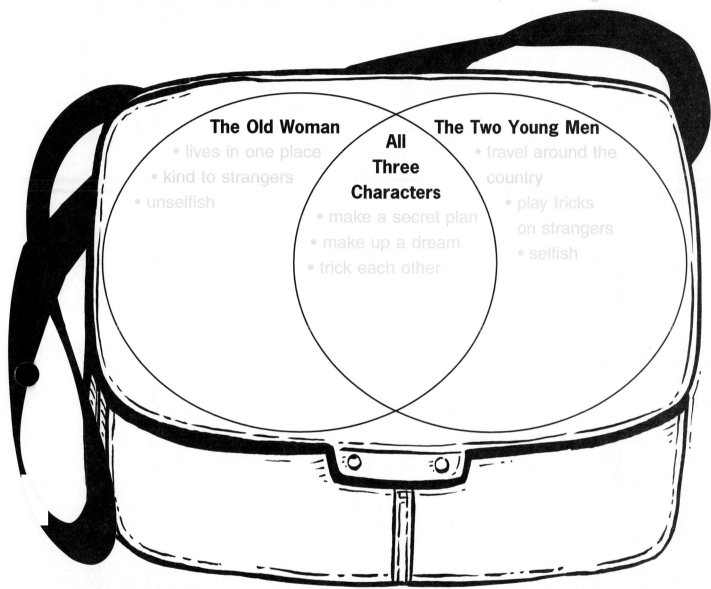

The Old Woman
• lives in one place
• kind to strangers
• unselfish

**All
Three
Characters**
• make a secret plan
• make up a dream
• trick each other

The Two Young Men
• travel around the
country
• play tricks
on strangers
• selfish

▶ **Briefly describe how the old woman manages to fool the young men.**

Possible response: She discovers they have stolen her ham. She replaces it

in their bag with an adobe brick. Later, when the men describe a fake dream

they had, she tells them her own fake dream about King Adobe. When the

men find the adobe brick later, they are surprised.

_____

Harcourt

Touch a Dream **127**

Name _____

▶ **Read each paragraph. Then follow the instructions and
answer the questions.** Exact wording may vary.

Wrap them around beans and cheese. Fill them with
chicken or beef. Eat them plain. What are they? Tortillas
(tor-TEE-yuhz)! Tortillas are a flat bread made of corn flour
or wheat flour. They have been a part of Mexican cooking for
hundreds of years. At first tortillas were made of corn kernels that
were boiled in a mixture of water and lime. The boiled kernels were
then ground into flour. The flour was dampened, patted into a pancake,
and baked on a griddle.

1. Write a paraphrase of the last sentence. The damp flour was made into a
   pancake and baked on a griddle.

2. Write a one-sentence summary of the paragraph. Tortillas are a traditional
   Mexican flat bread made of corn or wheat flour that are used with
   several kinds of food.

3. Write which of these sentences belongs in a good summary of the paragraph.
   a. Tortillas are delicious.
   b. Chicken or beef can be wrapped in a tortilla.
   c. Tortillas can be used in many different ways.

   Tortillas can be used in many different ways.

Although some people still make tortillas in the old way, many of today's
tortillas are machine-made. Machines grind the corn or wheat, shape the dough
into discs, and bake it. Sometimes machines even freeze the tortillas so they can
be stored for long periods of time.

4. Write a paraphrase of the first sentence. Some tortillas are still made in the
   traditional way, but now machines make many tortillas as well.

5. Write a one-sentence summary of the paragraph. Tortillas are made both
   by hand, using traditional methods, and by machine.

Harcourt

Name _____

▶ **Read the paragraph. Then read each question and choose the best answer. Mark the letter for that answer.**

If you enjoy eating tamales, thank the native peoples of Mexico. They were making tamales long before Spanish explorers arrived in the Americas. A favorite kind of tamale was made by wrapping a mixture of cornmeal and meat or fish in cornhusks. Tamales can have many different fillings. In some places a sweet version is popular.

1 Which of these sentences belongs in a summary of the paragraph?

   A Mexican restaurants serve tamales.

   B The native peoples ate corn and peppers.

   C Tamales are a tasty food.

   D The first tamales were made by native peoples in Mexico.

2 Which of these is a paraphrase of the first sentence?

   F Tamale fans can thank Mexico's native peoples.

   G If you enjoy eating tamales, thank the native peoples of Mexico.

   H People in Mexico like tamales made with a cornmeal filling.

   J There were people living in Mexico before the Spaniards came.

3 A good summary _____.

   A states the main ideas in a few words

   B is longer than the original

   C restates the original in your own words

   D includes many details

4 "Sweet tamales taste very strange." Why is this *not* a good paraphrase of the last sentence?

   F It is too short.

   G It gives only the main idea.

   H It does not restate the same information.

   J It gives unimportant details.

5 A paraphrase of a paragraph _____.

   A is very long

   B uses other words to restate the information

   C gives only a few details

   D tells only the main idea

Answers

1 Ⓐ Ⓑ Ⓒ Ⓓ
2 Ⓕ Ⓖ Ⓗ Ⓙ
3 Ⓐ Ⓑ Ⓒ Ⓓ
4 Ⓕ Ⓖ Ⓗ Ⓙ
5 Ⓐ Ⓑ Ⓒ Ⓓ

Harcourt

Name _____

▶ **Write a synonym for each underlined word in the sentences below. Use the words in the box.**

skinny	interested	stuffed	giving	mean
worst	increases	dishonest	boring	reckless

1. The young men were <u>full</u> after the delicious dinner.   _____ stuffed _____

2. The old woman was <u>thin</u> from lack of food.   _____ skinny _____

3. It is rare to find someone who is <u>generous</u> to strangers.   _____ giving _____

4. The children were <u>fascinated</u> to hear the old woman's stories.   _____ interested _____

5. The young men were <u>cruel</u> to steal food from a poor woman.   _____ mean _____

▶ **Write an antonym for each underlined word in the sentences below. Use the words in the box.**

6. She was an <u>honest</u> person in that story.   _____ dishonest _____

7. He is <u>careful</u> with garden tools.   _____ reckless _____

8. I always manage to pick the <u>best</u> piece of ham at Grandma's.   _____ worst _____

9. He <u>reduces</u> the number of prizes we can win each year.   _____ increases _____

10. The show was so <u>interesting</u> that we talked about it for a long time.   _____ boring _____

Harcourt

Name _____

▶ **Rewrite each sentence. Replace the blank with the type of adjective in parentheses ( ).** Responses will vary; possible responses are given.

1. The visitors described the _____ dreams. (**how many?**)

   The visitors described the three dreams. _____

   _____

2. It was a(n) _____ evening. (**what kind?**)

   It was a chilly evening. _____

   _____

3. The woman cooked _____ meal. (**which one?**)

   The woman cooked that meal. _____

   _____

4. Did _____ travelers learn a lesson? (**which ones?**)

   Did those travelers learn a lesson? _____

   _____

5. This was quite a(n) _____ adventure. (**what kind?**)

   This was quite an unusual adventure. _____

   _____

▶ **Rewrite each sentence, using the correct article in parentheses ( ).**

6. (**A, The**) travelers arrived at (**a, the**) old woman's house.

   The travelers arrived at the old woman's house. _____

7. Did they enjoy (**a, an**) exciting meal?

   Did they enjoy an exciting meal? _____

8. (**An, The**) ham was (**a, an**) big surprise!

   The ham was a big surprise! _____

Harcourt

▶ **Use the Spelling Words and the clues below to complete
the puzzle.**

Across

4. pay back
5. not busy
6. go back
9. not finished
10. consider again
11. containing no fat
12. took the place of

Down

1. say again
2. without stopping
3. not right
7. to make full again
8. read again

SPELLING WORDS

1. *nonstop*
2. *replaced*
3. *inactive*
4. *refill*
5. *incorrect*
6. *rethink*
7. *nonfat*
8. *reread*
9. *retell*
10. *return*
11. *incomplete*
12. *repay*

Across solutions shown in grid:
4. repay
5. inactive
6. return
9. incomplete
10. rethink
11. nonfat
12. replaced

Down solutions: 1. reread, 2. nonstop, 3. incorrect, 7. refill, 8. reread

Handwriting Tip: Use just one overjoining stroke when writing the
letter *n*, or it might look like *m*. Write the Spelling Words below.

inactive

13. return _____ return

15. incorrect _____ incorrect

14. inactive _____ inactive

16. incomplete _____ incomplete

 SCHOOL-HOME CONNECTION With your child, think of three
more words that have prefixes or suffixes. Then use the words in
sentences.

Harcourt

Name _____

▶ **Write a word from the box to complete each sentence.
Some words will be used twice.**

| script | triumphantly | desperately | injustice |
| repentant | acceptable | discards | circumstances |

Blue Grass **(1)** _____desperately_____ wants to change sad songs

into happy ones. First, he **(2)** _____discards_____ any songs

that make him cry. Then, he replaces them with songs that have

happy endings and are **(3)** _____acceptable_____ to him.

With these new **(4)** _____circumstances_____, he declares

(5) _____triumphantly_____ to his audience that they will go

home happy when they hear his songs.

But then an offer comes to him to write a sad song for a movie

(6) _____script_____! He knows this movie song would make him

famous. He thinks, "What an **(7)** _____injustice_____ — to become

famous for writing a sad song!" He **(8)** _____discards_____ the movie offer

and continues writing happy songs.

But he worries that he may be **(9)** _____repentant_____ about this

decision. He is very confused. He **(10)** _____desperately_____ wants to be a

famous songwriter.

Finally, a friend tells him there are many kinds of beautiful songs. He

knows what to do now under these **(11)** _____circumstances_____. He

(12) _____triumphantly_____ writes all kinds of songs that people can enjoy

in different ways.

SCHOOL-HOME CONNECTION Retell a favorite fairy tale or
other story with your child. Change the plot so that the ending is
completely different. Use at least three Vocabulary Words.

Touch a Dream **133**

Harcourt

Name _____

Skill Reminder	summary = main idea and details

paraphrase = the same information stated in other words

▶ **Read the paragraph. Then answer the questions.**

Exact wording will vary but should include the points listed below.

Do you ever play alphabet games and need a word that begins with *z*? If you're tired of *zoo* and *zebra*, next time try *zither*. A zither is a stringed musical instrument. It looks a little bit like a harp that's lying down. Zithers have anywhere from 29 to 42 strings. To play, you pluck the strings with the fingers of both hands. Many hundreds of years ago, the Greeks played an instrument called a *cithara*. The zither probably developed from the cithara. Zithers aren't very common anymore, but they were popular in the United States during the 1800s.

1. Write a short summary of the paragraph.

   The zither is a stringed musical instrument that was popular in the United

   States in the 1800s and that probably developed from an instrument

   called a cithara.

   _____

   _____

2. Write a paraphrase of the last sentence of the paragraph.

   Not many people play the zither anymore, but zithers were popular in the

   United States during the nineteenth century.

   _____

TRY THIS! Make a list of the events that took place as you came to school today. Then write a one-sentence summary based on your list.

Harcourt

Name _____

▶ **Before you read, fill in the prediction chart by writing what you think will happen. After you read, write what actually happens.**

Possible responses are given.

What I Predict Will Happen	What Actually Happens
The wolf will eat Red Writing Hood and her grandmother.	The wolf becomes a ballet dancer.
A spider will frighten away Miss Muffet.	A prince invites Miss Muffet to his palace.
Goldilocks will run away from the three bears.	The bears adopt Goldilocks.
Bo Peep won't find her lost sheep.	Red Writing Hood creates fifty sheep for Bo Peep.

▶ **Why does Red Writing Hood wish to change the fairy tales and nursery rhymes? Think about the kind of person she is.**

Possible response: She doesn't like stories in which people become sad or

get hurt. She likes only happy endings.

_____

Harcourt

Name _____

▶ **Write the letter of a good strategy to use from the box to find the meaning of each underlined word. Then write the meaning of the word from the choices given.**

A. **Look for a prefix or a suffix.**

B. **Think about the meaning of the base word.**

C. **See if the word is a compound word.**

Have you read the fairy tale about the elves who helped the <u>shoemaker</u>?

1. Strategy: _____ C _____

2. *Shoemaker* means _____ a person who makes shoes _____.

    a kind of shoe   **making tools**   **a person who makes shoes**

The man was so poor that it was <u>impossible</u> for him to buy leather for more shoes.

3. Strategy: _____ A _____

4. *Impossible* means _____ not possible _____.

    possible   **not possible**   **very likely**

One morning, to his astonishment, he found a perfectly made pair of shoes. He had no idea who his <u>mysterious</u> helpers were.

5. Strategy: (Responses may vary.) A or B

6. *Mysterious* means _____ full of mystery _____.

    full of mystery   **without mystery**   **too much mystery**

Imagine his <u>disbelief</u> when he discovered the elves at work!

7. Strategy: _____ A _____

8. *Disbelief* means _____ the opposite of belief _____.

    full of belief   **believable**   **the opposite of belief**

SCHOOL-HOME CONNECTION With your child, start a collection of long words that you hear or see in print. Talk about each word's pronunciation and meaning.

136 Touch a Dream

Harcourt

▶ **Rewrite each sentence, using the correct form of the adjective in parentheses ( ).**

1. Red whistled a _____ tune. **(joyful)**

   Red whistled a joyful tune. _____

2. It was a _____ tune than the one she whistled yesterday. **(happy)**

   It was a happier tune than the one she whistled yesterday. _____

3. In fact, it was the _____ tune she had whistled all week. **(nice)**

   In fact, it was the nicest tune she had whistled all week. _____

4. The wolf was looking forward to a _____ treat. **(tasty)**

   The wolf was looking forward to a tasty treat. _____

5. "These are the _____ berries I've ever had," he grinned. **(fine)**

   "These are the finest berries I've ever had," he grinned. _____

6. "Strawberries are _____ than blueberries," he declared. **(sweet)**

   "Strawberries are sweeter than blueberries," he declared. _____

▶ **Complete each sentence by writing the correct form of *good* in the blank.**

7. Making the wolf a ballet dancer

   was _____better_____ than having
   him visit Grandma's house.

8. Miss Muffet thought the new

   ending was the _____best_____
   she had heard.

Harcourt

TRY THIS! Imagine that your three favorite story characters could meet. Write a conversation they might have. Use several adjectives that compare. Exchange conversations with a classmate, and discuss the adjectives you used.

Name _____

▶ **Write the Spelling Word that means the opposite of each word or phrase.**

SPELLING WORDS

1. families
2. worried
3. ugliest
4. funnier
5. happily
6. easily
7. heavier
8. earlier
9. tiniest
10. supplied
11. luckily
12. relied

1. with difficulty _____easily_____

2. sadly _____happily_____

3. lighter _____heavier_____

4. prettiest _____ugliest_____

5. hugest _____tiniest_____

6. later _____earlier_____

▶ **Write a Spelling Word to complete each sentence.**

Five **(7)** _____families_____ met at the park.

Each family **(8)** _____supplied_____ some food.

Dad and I **(9)** _____worried_____ that it might rain.

Mom **(10)** _____relied_____ on the weather report.

(11) _____Luckily_____, the weather report was correct and it didn't rain. We all told funny stories.

My story was **(12)** _____funnier_____ than all the others.

Handwriting Tip: When you write the letter combination *lie*, be sure that only the *l* reaches the top writing line. Write the Spelling Words below.

earlier

13. families _____families_____   15. earlier _____earlier_____

14. ugliest _____ugliest_____   16. supplied _____supplied_____

Harcourt

▶ **Write a word from the box to complete each analogy.**

decreed	famine	implored	trickle	plentifully

1. *Singer* is to *chanted* as *beggar* is to ___implored___.

2. *Reward* is to *punishment* as *feast* is to ___famine___.

3. *Teacher* is to *instructed* as *king* is to ___decreed___.

4. *Enormous* is to *tiny* as *flood* is to ___trickle___.

5. *Quick* is to *quickly* as *plentiful* is to ___plentifully___.

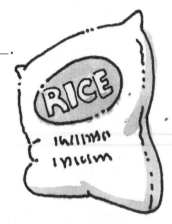

▶ **Write the word that matches each clue.**

6. This happens when there's no food. ___famine___

7. A judge did this. ___decreed___

8. It's how generous people give gifts. ___plentifully___

9. Someone in need did this. ___implored___

10. It's in a mostly dried-up stream. ___trickle___

TRY THIS! Make up your own folktale about a grain of rice. Include at least two Vocabulary Words.

Harcourt

Name _____

▶ **Complete the sequence chart below by writing important story events in the boxes.** Possible responses are given.

Important Events During Rani's Thirty Days

Date	Event
first day	She receives a single grain of rice.
second day	She receives two more grains of rice.
ninth day	She receives 256 grains of rice.
twentieth day	She receives 16 more bags of rice.
twenty-fourth day	She receives 8,388,608 grains of rice.
twenty-ninth day	She receives the contents of two royal storehouses.
thirtieth day	She receives 536,870,912 grains of rice.

▶ **Use the information in your time line to figure out how many grains of rice Rani would have received on the thirty-second day. Explain how you got your answer.** Wording may vary.

On Day 30 she received 536,870,912 grains of rice. Doubling that amount for

Day 31, she would get 1,073,741,824 grains. Doubling this amount for Day

32, she would get 2,147,483,648 grains.

Harcourt

▶ **On the lines, write the answers to the questions.**

Exact wording may vary.

More than half of India's land is used for farming. Its main products are rice, wheat, sugarcane, tea, and cotton. Rice is the main food eaten by much of the population.

1. Is the paragraph objective or subjective? _____ objective _____

2. How can you tell? The author gives facts and not opinions. The author doesn't try to get readers to believe any particular way.

Last September, I spent seven days in New Delhi, India. It poured rain on all seven days. I think that it must rain every day in India.

3. Is the paragraph objective or subjective? _____ subjective _____

4. How can you tell? The author gives facts but then draws a conclusion.

_____

5. The author says that it must rain every day in India. Is this conclusion valid?

Explain. no; The paragraph does not give enough information to prove

that it rains every day.

The national soccer team lost to Brazil yesterday by the score of 3–2. We have a terrible team this year. We have already lost three games.

6. Is the paragraph objective or subjective? _____ subjective _____

7. How can you tell? The author expresses an opinion, in addition to giving

facts.

Brazil, a top-ranked team, barely outscored our national soccer team yesterday by the score of 3–2. We can be proud of our team, which has won eight games this year while losing only three.

8. Is the paragraph objective or subjective? Explain. _____ subjective;

The author expresses his opinion throughout.

TRY THIS! Write a paragraph about a real or imaginary sports event. Choose words so the home team seems to be either a good or bad team.

Name _____

▶ **Write each underlined word beside the correct definition below.**

Rick's skin was very <u>fair</u>, so he put on a lot of sunblock.

Mrs. Morse kept the <u>deed</u> to her land locked in a safe.

Leah received a <u>reward</u> for finding the lost cat.

Martha could <u>double</u> her money if she worked all summer.

The ruler kept a huge <u>store</u> of rice hidden away.

The girl wasn't sure her <u>scheme</u> would work.

The ruler <u>declared</u> that all the people could share the wealth.

When the others <u>barred</u> the girl from entering the palace, the ruler let her in.

The ruler <u>scrutinized</u> the plan and decided it would work.

The girl was <u>overjoyed</u>, so she celebrated.

1. ____scrutinized____ looked over carefully

2. ____reward____ money given for the return of lost property

3. ____scheme____ plan

4. ____deed____ a legal document

5. ____store____ a supply of things put away for later use

6. ____overjoyed____ very happy

7. ____declared____ stated

8. ____fair____ light-colored

9. ____barred____ stopped

10. ____double____ make twice as much

Harcourt

SCHOOL-HOME CONNECTION Help your child find three new words in a dictionary. Then help him or her use the new words in sentences.

▶ **Underline the complete predicate in each sentence, and circle the verb. On the line, write *action* or *being* to identify the verb.**

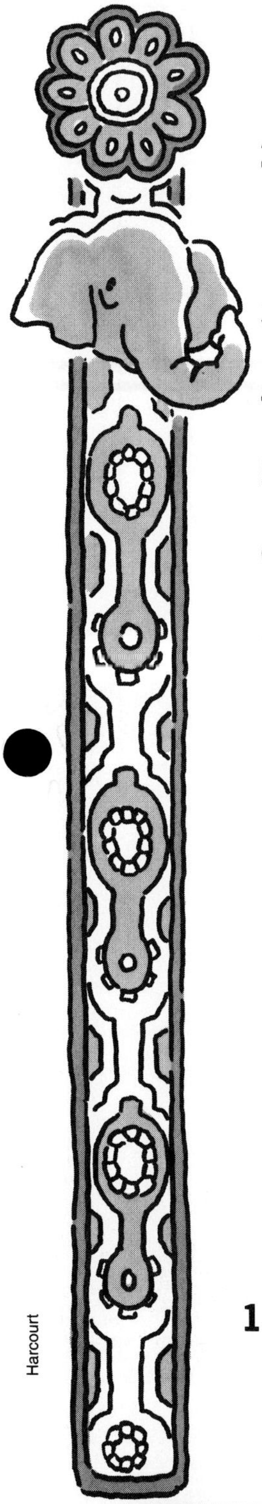

1. China and India ⟨are⟩ the biggest producers of rice in the world. ___being___

2. Farmers in Arkansas, California, Texas, and Louisiana ⟨grow⟩ a lot of rice, too. ___action___

3. Rice plants ⟨thrive⟩ in 4 to 8 inches of water. ___action___

4. Actually, rice ⟨is⟩ the fruit of a type of grass. ___being___

5. Harvesters ⟨remove⟩ rice grains from the plant. ___action___

6. At the mill, workers ⟨process⟩ the rice. ___action___

▶ **Underline the verb or verb group in each sentence. Then write a new sentence using the verb or verb group you underlined.** New sentences will vary.

7. Bran, a thin brown skin, covers rice. _____

_____

8. Brown rice has many vitamins and minerals. _____

_____

9. The bran is removed at the mill. _____

_____

10. The kernels are polished for white rice. _____

_____

TRY THIS! Rani used mathematics to feed the people. Write five sentences about ways people use mathematics. Underline the verbs in your sentences.

Harcourt

Name _____

▶ **Write the Spelling Word that matches each clue.**

1. answer _____solution_____

2. purpose _____function_____

3. more than enough _____plentiful_____

4. sorrow _____sadness_____

5. silence _____stillness_____

SPELLING WORDS
1. addition
2. sadness
3. lovable
4. endless
5. handful
6. plentiful
7. breathless
8. happiness
9. solution
10. careful
11. function
12. stillness

▶ **Add a suffix to the underlined word to write a Spelling Word.**

6. Put your <u>hand</u> into the jar and

   grab a _____handful_____ of rice.

7. We all <u>love</u> the new puppy. Boots is a

   _____lovable_____ little dog.

8. I thought that movie would never <u>end</u>.

   It seemed _____endless_____!

9. Do you like to <u>add</u>? Yes, _____addition_____ is my favorite part of math.

10. Take <u>care</u> when you ride your bike. It's important

    to be _____careful_____ on the road.

11. Jed grew short of <u>breath</u> as he ran. He was _____breathless_____.

12. Habib felt so <u>happy</u>! His _____happiness_____ showed in his wide grin.

Handwriting Tip: Keep your letter strokes smooth and steady. Do not go over your strokes again. Write the Spelling Words below.

13. addition _____addition_____   15. endless _____endless_____

14. sadness _____sadness_____   16. handful _____handful_____

Harcourt

▶ **Write a word from the water to best complete each sentence.**
Use some words twice. Possible answers are given.

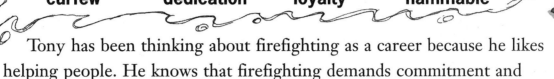

ventilate   billowing   brigade

curfew   dedication   loyalty   flammable

Tony has been thinking about firefighting as a career because he likes helping people. He knows that firefighting demands commitment and

(1) _____dedication_____. By nature he is a true friend, and he has shown his

(2) _____loyalty_____ by helping his friends solve their problems. Tony decided the best way to find out if he would like to be a firefighter would be to spend some time at his local fire station. But since his parents have set a

(3) _____curfew_____ for him, he would not be able to stay past 8:00 P.M. When Tony arrived, the firefighters explained how the first firefighting

(4) _____brigade_____ had formed long ago. They told him about the many

new inventions, such as clothing that is not **(5)** _____flammable_____, that help firefighters stay safe.

Tony told the firefighters that he knew smoke was dangerous. He had learned that he should crawl on his knees if caught in a fire. Since the smoke would be

(6) _____billowing_____ upward, the cleanest air would be near the floor. The firefighters said this is why they wear breathing masks. They have to

(7) _____ventilate_____ their lungs so they can stand up to work.

The firefighters also reminded Tony about outdoor fires and how quickly they can spread in a forest because wood is very

(8) _____flammable_____. Tony didn't want to leave but knew the time of his

(9) _____curfew_____ was getting near.

He was more impressed than ever with firefighters' **(10)** _____dedication_____

and **(11)** _____loyalty_____ to their jobs and to helping the community.

SCHOOL-HOME CONNECTION Talk with your child about fire-safety rules to observe both inside and outside your home. Use some Vocabulary Words.

Touch a Dream   **145**

Harcourt

Name _____

Skill Reminder   Manage your time. Skip questions you don't know.

▶ Write the test-taking strategies from the box in the order that they should be followed.

Return to questions I skipped.	Check my answers.
Look over the whole test.	Answer questions I know first.
Read directions carefully.	

1. First: _Look over the whole test._

2. Next: _Read directions carefully._

3. Then: _Answer questions I know first._

4. Then: _Return to questions I skipped._

5. Last: _Check my answers._

▶ Write the answer to the question from the choices below. Then write the letter of the strategies you used. Strategies may vary.

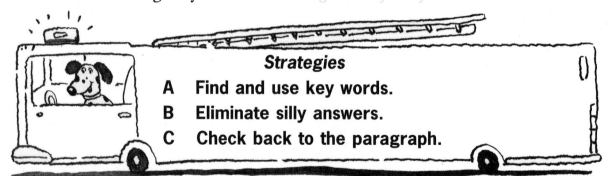

Strategies
A Find and use key words.
B Eliminate silly answers.
C Check back to the paragraph.

Dalmatians are spotted dogs that have been popular with fire departments for over 100 years. These dogs were able to run along with horse-drawn fire engines without getting kicked accidentally by the horses. Even when motorized fire trucks came along, Dalmatians stayed on as fire department mascots.

6. What special ability do Dalmatians have?

_____ running with horses without getting kicked; A, B, C _____

fighting fires   **running behind horses without getting kicked**

Harcourt

Name _____

▶ **Fill in the first two columns of the K-W-L chart. Then use information from the story to fill in the last column.** Possible responses are given.

What I **K**now	What I **W**ant to Know	What I **L**earned
Firefighters put out fires.	How do firefighters fight fires?	They use hoses and they break windows to ventilate buildings.
Firefighters ride on trucks and wear special outfits.	What kind of clothes and equipment do firefighters use?	They wear helmets, masks, bunker pants, boots, and gloves. They use pressure gauges, air cylinders, and walkie-talkies.
Firefighters rescue people and animals in trouble.	What is a firefighter's day like?	Firefighters may sleep and eat at the station. They attend training sessions. Sometimes they get a call to rescue a child locked in a bathroom, or help a cat stuck inside a wall.

▶ **Write a one-sentence summary of the whole selection.**

Possible response: Fighting fires involves firefighters who are trained to use

special equipment and who are deeply committed to their jobs.

Harcourt

▶ **Read the paragraph. Then write three facts from the paragraph on the top fire truck and three opinions from the paragraph on the bottom fire truck.** Exact wording may vary.

A student who is studying to be an emergency medical technician, or EMT, in Dallas must work a 24-hour shift at a fire station. The students go with firefighters who answer calls for medical help. This is the most exciting part of EMT training. It's a real thrill to ride on the ambulance through the city streets! Sometimes they give first aid to someone who is injured. Providing emergency medical care is a hard job.

1. A student who is studying to be an emergency medical technician in Dallas must work a 24-hour shift at a fire station.

2. The students go with firefighters who answer calls for medical help.

3. Sometimes they give first aid to someone who is injured.

Facts

4. This is the most exciting part of EMT training.

5. It's a real thrill to ride on the ambulance through the city streets!

6. Providing emergency medical care is a hard job.

Opinions

TRY THIS! Look at the illustration of the firefighter's turnout gear in "Fire!" Write your opinion of how it would feel to wear that gear.

Harcourt

Name _____

▶ **Read the passage. Then read each question and decide which is the best answer. Mark the letter for that answer.**

Some people like to work for no money at all! Every summer many students do volunteer work. Some work in hospitals. The most rewarding job there is working with children. Volunteers read to children and play with them. Volunteers do other jobs, too, such as helping in the hospital offices. Hospital volunteer work is a good way to spend the summer. It is not boring at all.

There are many volunteer organizations. Working for your community is a wonderful job. Everyone should try it. You can ask your local hospital for an application. Or you can volunteer at another place. You won't be sorry.

1 Which sentence is an opinion?

A Some people like to work for no money at all!

B Every summer many students do volunteer work.

C Some work in hospitals.

D Hospital volunteer work is a good way to spend the summer.

2 Which sentence is a fact?

F The most rewarding job is working with children.

G Volunteers read to children and play with them.

H Hospital volunteer work is a good way to spend the summer.

J It is not boring at all.

3 Which sentence is an opinion?

A There are many volunteer organizations.

B Everyone should try it.

C You can ask your local hospital for an application.

D Or you can volunteer at another place.

4 Which sentence is a fact?

F Working for your community is a wonderful job.

G Everyone should try it.

H You can ask your local hospital for an application.

J You won't be sorry.

Answers

1 Ⓐ Ⓑ Ⓒ Ⓓ

2 Ⓕ Ⓖ Ⓗ Ⓙ

3 Ⓐ Ⓑ Ⓒ Ⓓ

4 Ⓕ Ⓖ Ⓗ Ⓙ

Harcourt

▶ Use the book cover, table of contents, glossary, and index
to answer the questions on the next page.

Fighting the Blaze
by James and Sandra Boyd

**True Stories of Firefighters
in All 50 States**

Table of Contents

Glossary

alarm: a bell or siren used to give a
   warning
brigade: a group of people organized
   for a certain purpose
paramedic units: groups that give
   emergency first aid on the scene
pumper: a truck that carries a pump
   and hoses for spraying water on a
   fire
smoke detector: a device that
   sounds an alarm if there is smoke
   in a room

Index

Harcourt

GO ON

Name _____

▶ **Write your answer to each question. Then write the name of the book part where you found each answer.**

1. What is the title of the book? _____Fighting the Blaze_____

   Book part: _____book cover_____

2. How many chapters does the book have? _____four_____

   Book part: _____table of contents_____

3. On what page does the third chapter begin? _____page 59_____

   Book part: _____table of contents_____

4. What is a *pumper*? _____a truck that carries a pump and water hoses_____

   Book part: _____glossary_____

5. What page mentions Little Rock, Arkansas? _____page 100_____

   Book part: _____index_____

6. Which pages mention an airport crash truck? _____pages 63 and 65_____

   Book part: _____index_____

7. Who are the authors of the book? _____James and Sandra Boyd_____

   Book part: _____book cover_____

8. Which chapter has stories about pets? _____Chapter two_____

   Book part: _____table of contents_____

9. What are *paramedic units*? _____groups that give emergency first aid on the scene_____

   Book part: _____glossary_____

10. Which cities in California are mentioned? _____Los Angeles and San Diego_____

    Book part: _____index_____

Name _____

▶ **Write a word from the list to complete each sentence.**

worker   a call into the station, requiring the fire
truck and firefighters to go out

bunker   type of pants tucked into rubber boots

overhaul   to remove cinders and anything that
might burn and to soak the area with water

rekindle   to restart

dispatch   the switchboard that takes incoming calls

turnout   firefighting gear

knocked down   completely put out

back-stepper   an old-fashioned term for *firefighter*

1. The crew jumped on the truck and headed out

when the _____worker_____ came in.

2. An urgent phone call came in to the _____dispatch_____ operator.

3. Tim found an old newspaper picture of a _____back-stepper_____
putting out a fire.

4. It took five hours, but finally the fire was _____knocked down_____.

5. The crew grabbed all of their _____turnout_____ before jumping
on the fire truck.

6. They stayed behind at the scene of the fire to make sure the fire did not

_____rekindle_____.

7. He always sets out his _____bunker_____ pants before going to sleep
at the fire station.

8. The chief made every person on the crew work to carefully

_____overhaul_____ the fire scene.

TRY THIS! Read in a reference book about another interesting profession. Research
the special terms used in that profession.

Harcourt

Name _____

▶ **Underline the main verb. Circle the helping verb.**

1. The children have opened the hydrant.

2. Water is pouring all over the ground.

3. Their game could prove dangerous.

4. Perhaps the water will dry up.

5. Then any fire would cause
great damage.

▶ **Complete each sentence. Use a verb from the box. Then circle the helping verb.**

take	deserve	extinguished	relaxing	answer

6. The firefighters were _____ relaxing .

7. They had _____ extinguished a fire early that morning.

8. They do _____ deserve a break now.

9. One firefighter will _____ answer the phones.

10. The rest should _____ take a nap.

TRY THIS! On a separate sheet of paper, write five sentences about fighting fires. Use one of these helping verbs in each sentence: *were could does has will*

Touch a Dream **153**

Harcourt

▶ **Write the Spelling Word that names each picture.**

1. _____ collar

3. _____ dollar

2. _____ ladder

4. _____ corner

SPELLING WORDS
1. doctor
2. dollar
3. power
4. sugar
5. corner
6. collar
7. danger
8. ladder
9. labor
10. cellar
11. other
12. motor

▶ **The letters of the underlined words are mixed up. Write the correct Spelling Words on the lines.**

5. The <u>rtoom</u> of the fire engine is huge. _____ motor

6. The firefighters drink coffee with <u>agusr</u> in it for energy. _____ sugar

7. Smoke is coming from the <u>clrale</u>. _____ cellar

8. The firefighters and a <u>rooctd</u> are on the way. _____ doctor

9. Is there any <u>radnge</u> of an explosion? _____ danger

10. It will take hard <u>boarl</u> to break down that cellar door. _____ labor

11. Water shoots from a fire hose with tremendous <u>worep</u>. _____ power

12. Should we call for any <u>hotre</u> kinds of help? _____ other

Handwriting Tip: When you connect the vowels *a*, *o*, and *e* to *r*, make sure the *r* does not look like an *i*. Write the Spelling Words below.

13. sugar _____ sugar

15. labor _____ labor

14. corner _____ corner

16. doctor _____ doctor

Harcourt

Name _____

▶ Write the word from the box that matches each clue. The
message in the shaded area of the answers tells you what
a person may become on an important day.

apologized	obliged	certificate	examiner
petitioners	resounded	enrich	

1. an official document   c e r t i f i **c** a t e

2. one who gives a test   e x a m **i** n e r

3. people asking for something   p e t i **t** i o n e r s

4. to make better   e n r **i** c h

5. said "I'm sorry"   a p o l o g i **z** e d

6. did what was wanted   o b l i **g** e d

7. echoed   r e s o u **n** d e d

▶ Write the word that answers each riddle.

8. I am an important piece of paper.
What am I?   __certificate__

9. We are requesting something.
Who are we?   __petitioners__

10. I give exams.
Who am I?   __examiner__

I pledge allegiance to the flag . . .

 **TRY
THIS!** Write a paragraph telling what country your family came from and when.
Use at least three Vocabulary Words.

Harcourt

Name _____

Skill Reminder	Book Cover — title, author; Table of

Contents — chapter titles and page number where each
chapter begins; Glossary — definitions of words;
Index — page numbers of topics

▶ Read each question and the names of the book parts. Then write the name
of the book part where you could find the answer to each question.

Book Cover Table of Contents Glossary Index

1. Who wrote the book? _____Book Cover_____

2. What is the title of the first chapter? _____Table of Contents_____

3. On what page is Brooklyn mentioned? _____Index_____

4. What does the word *Constitution* mean? _____Glossary_____

5. On what page does the chapter "How
   to Become a Citizen" begin? _____Table of Contents_____

6. Which pages tell about immigration? _____Index_____

7. How many chapters does the book have? _____Table of Contents_____

8. What is a *borough*? _____Glossary_____

9. What pages tell about the Pledge of
   Allegiance? _____Index_____

10. What is the title of the book? _____Book Cover_____

TRY THIS! Look at several different magazines in your classroom and compare the
tables of contents. Do they all give the same information? In what ways are
they different?

Harcourt

Skill Reminder   Fact — can be supported by evidence
Opinion — states a belief, judgment, or feeling

▶ Write *fact* or *opinion* beside each sentence.

1. One of the best things about visiting New York City is a trip
   to Ellis Island. _____opinion_____

2. This is the place where more than 12 million immigrants entered the
   United States between 1892 and 1954. _____fact_____

3. The first one to pass through Ellis Island was a 15-year-old
   Irish girl named Annie Moore. _____fact_____

4. How exciting it must have been to
   arrive in America! _____opinion_____

5. Annie arrived on the steamship *Nevada*
   on January 1, 1892. _____fact_____

6. She came with her two younger brothers. _____fact_____

7. They were met by their parents, who had come to New York three years
   before. _____fact_____

8. Annie was the bravest girl alive. _____opinion_____

9. She must have truly wanted to be an American. _____opinion_____

10. Today there is a bronze statue of Annie on the second floor of the Ellis
    Island Immigration Museum. _____fact_____

TRY THIS!   Write a paragraph about someone you admire. Include both facts and
opinions. Label the facts *F* and the opinions *O*.

Name _____

▶ As you read, start to fill in the prediction web. After you
read, write what actually happens. Possible responses are given.

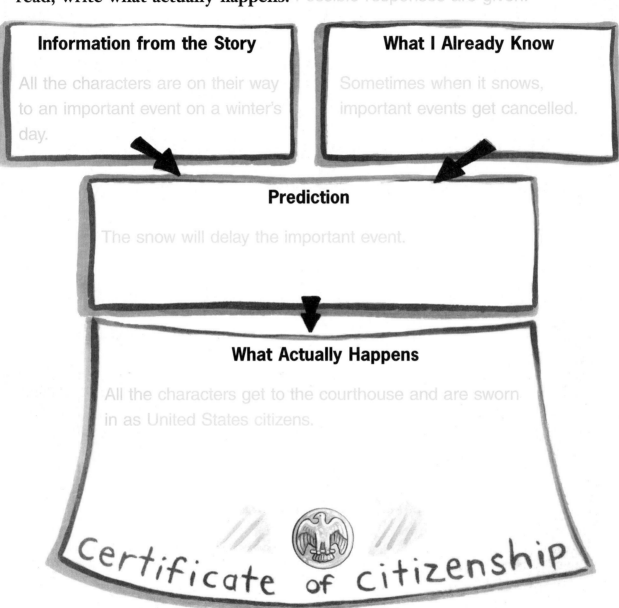

Information from the Story

All the characters are on their way
to an important event on a winter's
day.

What I Already Know

Sometimes when it snows,
important events get cancelled.

Prediction

The snow will delay the important event.

What Actually Happens

All the characters get to the courthouse and are sworn
in as United States citizens.

certificate of citizenship

▶ Explain why all the characters refer to the day as "a very important day."
What makes it so important to them?

Possible response: It is the day they become United States citizens. As

citizens, they can now vote, serve on juries, hold government jobs, travel

outside the United States, and sponsor other family members who wish to

live in the United States of America.

Harcourt

Name _____

▶ **Read the paragraph. Then write *valid* or *invalid* beside each generalization.**

When Hans arrived in the United States in 1907, he didn't speak English. At Ellis Island he stood in line with hundreds of other immigrants, waiting for permission to enter the country. How long the line was! How tired Hans felt after his long journey from Germany with his family! Hans and the others had to be examined by a doctor right away. If the doctor found any medical problems, then the immigrant had to be examined again by other doctors. Hans was very nervous. Sick children over the age of 12 could not leave Ellis Island to enter the United States. They had to go back across the ocean alone. Their parents and family did not return with them. Hans had just had his twelfth birthday. He hoped the doctor wouldn't notice his little cough.

Generalization	Valid or Invalid
1. Immigrants do not speak English.	invalid
2. Immigrants have illnesses.	invalid
3. Some immigrants weren't allowed to enter the United States.	valid
4. Sometimes immigrant children were separated from their parents.	valid
5. All immigrants were nervous.	invalid
6. Some immigrants came from Germany.	valid
7. Doctors worked at Ellis Island.	valid
8. Doctors were always cruel to the immigrants.	invalid
9. Children were always separated from their parents.	invalid
10. Sometimes families immigrated together.	valid

Harcourt

Name _____

▶ Homographs are words that are spelled the same but have different meanings and, often, different pronunciations. Write the word from the box that can replace both underlined words in the sentence.

desert	suspect	dove	extract
minute	records	wind	produce

1. The airplane <u>swooped</u> in order to miss the <u>bird</u>.   ___dove___

2. The <u>breeze</u> was so strong that Mark could not <u>tighten the spring</u> of the clock in the tower.   ___wind___

3. Lisa would not <u>leave</u> her friend Jan in the <u>hot, dry, sandy area</u>.   ___desert___

4. We could not <u>pull out</u> the part of the plant that is used to make vanilla <u>concentrate</u>.   ___extract___

5. It took only <u>sixty seconds</u> to dig down to the <u>tiny</u> roots of the plant.   ___minute___

6. The man <u>writes down</u> facts that become part of historical <u>documents</u>.   ___records___

7. I am beginning to <u>think it likely</u> that the <u>person under suspicion</u> is guilty.   ___suspect___

8. My garden can <u>grow</u> a large amount of <u>fruits and vegetables</u> if I use a special fertilizer.   ___produce___

vanilla

TRY THIS! List three other words that can be used in two ways. For each word, write a sentence that uses it with both meanings.

Harcourt

Name _____

▶ **Underline the verb. Tell what kind of verb it is. Write**
action **or** *linking*.

1. Citizens <u>say</u> the Pledge of Allegiance. ____action____

2. "I <u>pledge</u> allegiance to the flag." ____action____

3. The Pledge <u>is</u> an oath of loyalty. ____linking____

4. It <u>promises</u> devotion to the U.S.A. ____action____

5. Citizens <u>are</u> proud of their country. ____linking____

6. They gladly <u>share</u> in the ceremony. ____action____

7. The American flag <u>is</u> overhead. ____linking____

8. It <u>commands</u> everyone's attention. ____action____

▶ **Complete each sentence with the kind of verb in parentheses ( ).**
Responses will vary. Possible responses are given.

9. Fatima ____places____
   one hand on her heart. **(action)**

10. She ____seems____ very
    happy today. **(linking)**

11. Mr. Kao ____looks____
    at his new flag. **(action)**

12. He ____is____
    now an American. **(linking)**

Harcourt

SCHOOL-HOME CONNECTION Talk with your child about what being
a citizen means to him or her. With your child, write three sentences
that tell your family's ideas. Underline the verb in each sentence.

Name _____

▶ **Read the following paragraphs. Find and circle the twelve misspelled words. Then write each word correctly on the lines.**

Jorge turned the (handal) and opened the door. He took a (finle) look around. The room was quite (ushuel). Above the bed hung a (singal) picture he had painted. It was a (jungal) scene with a large (animle).

Jorge walked over to his (tabel). He picked up a (bottal) of soda and started to read his diary, the record of his (personel) thoughts. Then he opened an old book and looked at an (exampal) of his earliest handwriting.

He couldn't believe his trip was an (aktual) event. Was it (possibel) that he was going to move to another country?

SPELLING WORDS

1. table
2. final
3. handle
4. personal
5. animal
6. usual
7. jungle
8. actual
9. example
10. bottle
11. possible
12. single

1. _____handle_____   7. _____table_____

2. _____final_____   8. _____bottle_____

3. _____usual_____   9. _____personal_____

4. _____single_____   10. _____example_____

5. _____jungle_____   11. _____actual_____

6. _____animal_____   12. _____possible_____

Handwriting Tip: Be sure all letters slant in the same direction. Write the Spelling Words below.

final

13. handle _____handle_____   15. example _____example_____

14. actual _____actual_____   16. bottle _____bottle_____

Harcourt

Name _____

▶ **Write a word from the box to complete each sentence.**

| local | attic | gymnasium | installed | trolley | sweltering |

1. We went upstairs to the _____attic_____ to find our old roller skates.

2. The _____local_____ weather station didn't say how hot it would be today.

3. The house was _____sweltering_____, and I had to turn on the fan.

4. We ordered an air conditioner, but it hasn't been _____installed_____ yet.

5. Later, when it cools off, I'm going to the _____gymnasium_____ to work out.

6. When I leave, I'll ride the _____trolley_____ downtown.

▶ **Write the Vocabulary Word that best fits with each pair of words or phrases below.**

7. top floor   storage space
   _____attic_____

8. put in   fixed in place
   _____installed_____

9. neighborhood   town
   _____local_____

10. bus   train
    _____trolley_____

11. hot   humid
    _____sweltering_____

12. sports   arena
    _____gymnasium_____

▶ **Write the Vocabulary Word that means the *opposite* of each clue below.**

13. cold   _____sweltering_____

14. taken out   _____installed_____

15. worldwide   _____local_____

16. cellar   _____attic_____

TRY THIS! Describe the houses or apartments in your neighborhood. Use at least three Vocabulary Words.

Harcourt

Name _____

▶ As you read "House, House," fill in the Venn diagram to describe the city of Hatfield, then and now.
Possible responses are given.

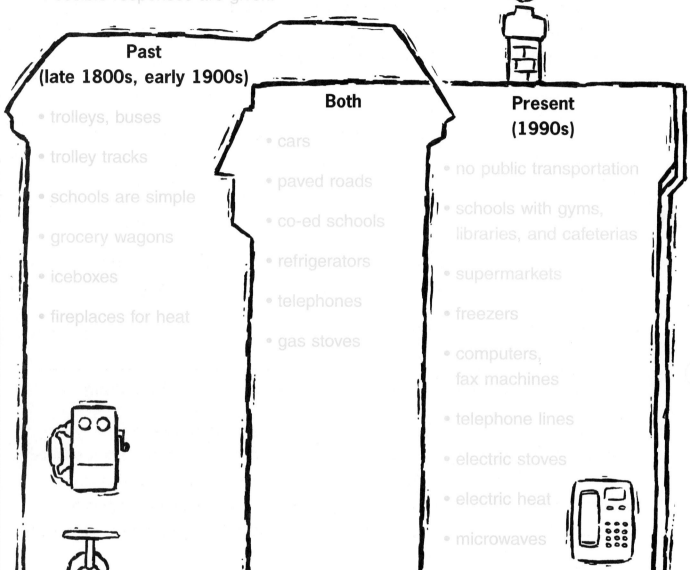

Past
(late 1800s, early 1900s)

• trolleys, buses

• trolley tracks

• schools are simple

• grocery wagons

• iceboxes

• fireplaces for heat

Both

• cars

• paved roads

• co-ed schools

• refrigerators

• telephones

• gas stoves

Present
(1990s)

• no public transportation

• schools with gyms, libraries, and cafeterias

• supermarkets

• freezers

• computers, fax machines

• telephone lines

• electric stoves

• electric heat

• microwaves

• air conditioning

▶ As you look at the houses and their surroundings in this selection, describe the changes you see.

Possible response: style of doors, windows changed; shutters added or

taken off; porches added or taken off; some additions to houses made;

shrubbery added; some large trees cut down; cars in present-day driveways.

Harcourt

Name _____

▶ **Read each paragraph and answer the questions. Choose from the words or phrases below.**

Everyone should support the mayor's efforts to have a citywide cleanup day this spring. We can pick up trash and cut the grass in our park. The wooden play area there needs a coat of paint. The fence needs to be repaired. Some of these projects cost money, but it will be money well spent. A clean, neat park is important. Let's show our pride and clean up our park and our city!

1. The author wants to _____persuade_____ readers.

    entertain   **inform**   **persuade**

2. The author thinks that cleanup day is a _____good_____ idea.

    good   **bad**   **strange**

3. Probably this author thinks that people should _____spend more money on parks_____.

    spend more money on parks   **try to save money**   **do nothing**

Having a citywide cleanup day is not a good idea. Much of the painting and other work that our park needs can be paid for by private donations. We should not spend the city's money this way. The money should be spent on street repair instead. Our city's streets are a disgrace. They are bumpy, and some of the holes are large enough to be dangerous. Smooth streets are important for the comfort and safety of everyone in our city.

4. The author wants to _____persuade_____ readers.

    entertain   **inform**   **persuade**

5. The author believes that a cleanup day is a _____bad_____ idea.

    good   **bad**   **strange**

6. The author probably thinks that _____safety is an issue_____.

    the parks are clean enough   **safety is an issue**   **cities are clean**

TRY THIS! Look back at the selection "Fire!" Write what you think is the author's point of view about firefighting. List the details that help you know this.

Harcourt

▶ **Read the paragraph. Then choose the answer that best completes each sentence. Mark the letter for that answer.**

Farm families did not have an easy life in the 1920s. Everyone worked, even the children. Older children worked with the farmhands in the fields, and younger children had chores to do around the house. There was little time for play, and many families had no money for anything more than food and clothing. Days began early, with farm chores to do even before the sun rose. Long days of struggle, trying to raise a large enough crop to support the family, were tiring and not always rewarding.

1 This author probably _____.

A would like to have lived in the country in the 1920s

B is glad not to be living on a farm in the 1920s

C enjoys farm chores

D would have liked to be a farmer

2 The author's purpose is probably to _____.

F entertain

G persuade

H entertain and to persuade

J inform

3 The author probably wants readers to _____.

A forget all about life long ago

B move to the country

C appreciate farm families who lived hard lives

D learn how to grow crops

4 The author would probably agree that _____.

F farm life was great fun

G farm life was hard and uncomfortable

H more people should live on farms

J life was better in the 1920s than it is now.

5 The author's perspective may depend on _____.

A whether he has ever lived on a farm

B where he went on vacation

C where his ancestors came from

D how big his family is

Answers

1 Ⓐ ● Ⓒ Ⓓ
2 Ⓕ Ⓖ Ⓗ Ⓙ
3 Ⓐ Ⓑ Ⓒ Ⓓ
4 Ⓕ Ⓖ Ⓗ Ⓙ
5 Ⓐ Ⓑ Ⓒ Ⓓ

Harcourt

Name _____

▶ **Write the best reference source for finding each answer. Choose from the sources shown below.**

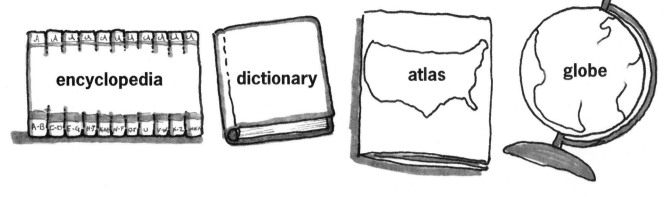

encyclopedia   dictionary   atlas   globe

1. What interstate highways pass through Houston, Texas?

   _____ atlas _____

2. What is the correct pronunciation of the word *literacy*?

   _____ dictionary _____

3. Which South American countries are north of the equator?

   _____ globe or atlas _____

4. Where were the first public libraries built?

   _____ encyclopedia _____

5. For what work is Horace Mann best known?

   _____ encyclopedia _____

6. What does the word *bandwagon* mean?

   _____ dictionary _____

7. What place is on the exact opposite part of the earth from where you live?

   _____ globe _____

8. How far is it from Dallas to New Orleans?

   _____ atlas _____

9. What are the main crops grown in Oklahoma?

   _____ encyclopedia _____

10. What is the origin of the word *boondoggle*?

   _____ dictionary _____

Harcourt

Name _____

▶ **Help Darcy complete her report on national parks.**
Write the entry word or words she should look up in an encyclopedia to
find the information she needs. Answers may vary.

1. What did President Theodore Roosevelt do about national parks?

    _____Roosevelt, Theodore; national parks_____

2. Where is Yellowstone National Park located?

    _____Yellowstone; national parks_____

3. How is a canyon formed?

    _____canyon_____

4. What is the country's largest national park?

    _____national parks_____

5. Who was John Muir?

    _____Muir, John_____

6. What are some tips for good photography in national parks?

    _____photography_____

7. How deep is the Grand Canyon?

    _____Grand Canyon_____

8. What was Denali National Park called in the past?

    _____Denali_____

9. Who first explored Carlsbad Caverns?

    _____Carlsbad Caverns_____

10. Who built the cliff dwellings at Mesa Verde National Park?

    _____Mesa Verde; cliff dwellings_____

TRY THIS! Read a magazine article or a nonfiction selection in a book. Make a list of questions you have about the topic. Beside each, write the entry word or words you would look up in an encyclopedia to find the answer.

Harcourt

Name _____

▶ **Rewrite these sentences
by using the correct
present-tense form of the word in parentheses ( ).**

1. The street **(is, was)** lined with beautiful trees.

   The street is lined with beautiful trees.
   _____

2. This house is so big that it **(look, looks)** like a mansion.

   This house is so big that it looks like a mansion.
   _____

3. All the houses **(has, have)** large front yards.

   All the houses have large front yards.
   _____

4. He **(go, goes)** to the school down the street.

   He goes to the school down the street.
   _____

▶ **Write the present-tense form of the verb in parentheses ( ) to complete
each sentence.**

5. The small car _____makes_____ the garage look huge. **(make)**

6. New cars _____cost_____ a lot of money. **(cost)**

7. The dog _____passes_____ the boy on their way home. **(pass)**

8. The boy _____hurries_____ to get on the porch first. **(hurry)**

9. Telephone lines _____run_____ through the community. **(run)**

10. We will need help when we _____build_____ our new house. **(build)**

11. The writer _____works_____ hard at her craft. **(work)**

12. The photographer _____tries_____ to take good pictures. **(try)**

**TRY
THIS!** Using only present-tense verbs, write a paragraph describing what you see on
your way to school. Then rewrite the paragraph by using the plural subject *we.*

Harcourt

▶ **Write the Spelling Word that fits each clue.**

1. load _____ burden

2. summer _____ season

3. rhymes with *Steven* _____ even

4. having to do with cities _____ urban

5. cause _____ reason

6. person _____ human

SPELLING WORDS
1. woman
2. even
3. urban
4. seven
5. kitchen
6. reason
7. human
8. season
9. burden
10. wagon
11. oven
12. dragon

▶ **Write the Spelling Word that names each picture.**

7. _____ seven

10. _____ woman

8. _____ kitchen

11. _____ dragon

9. _____ oven

12. _____ wagon

Handwriting Tip: When you write the letter combination *on*, take care to keep the joining stroke high. Otherwise, the letters may look like *an*. Write the Spelling Words below.

13. reason _____ reason

15. wagon _____ wagon

14. season _____ season

16. dragon _____ dragon

Harcourt

▶ **Write words from the box to replace the underlined words.**

sulkily	indifferent	protruded	loathe
undoubtedly	heartily	certainty	

I had thought that I was going to hate **(1)** _____loathe_____ Camp

Miller School. Was I wrong! I frowned angrily **(2)** _____sulkily_____

all the way there on my first day. But Miss Peterson was so nice! She is surely

(3) _____undoubtedly_____ the best teacher in all the camp schools. I no

longer felt disinterested **(4)** _____indifferent_____ about school. My teacher

greeted me in a warm and friendly way **(5)** _____heartily_____ .

I now feel with sureness **(6)** _____certainty_____ that I will like

the school after all. The pouting lower lip that once pushed out

(7) _____protruded_____ from my face has curved into a smile!

▶ **Use each pair of words in one sentence.** Responses will vary.

8. indifferent   heartily

_____Possible response: Joanne's parents were surprised when she welcomed_____

_____her cousin heartily, since she had seemed indifferent about his visit._____

9. sulkily   loathe

_____Possible response: As the class started reading *Willy Wonka and the*_____

_____*Chocolate Factory*, Susan muttered sulkily, "I loathe chocolate."_____

10. undoubtedly   indifferent

_____Possible response: My brother will undoubtedly be indifferent to our plans._____

TRY THIS! Write about yourself on the first day of a new school year. Tell what happens and how you felt about it. Use at least three Vocabulary Words.

Harcourt

Name _____

Author's Purpose and Perspective

| Skill Reminder | purpose = entertain, inform, or persuade |
| | perspective = opinions or attitude |

Science

▶ **Read each paragraph. Then write your answer from the choices of words or phrases to complete each sentence.**

Rafael's Report

The horned toad is an animal that nobody could possibly want to touch. It looks scary, with horns on its head and sharp spines all over its body. It has a mean glare when it looks at someone who has disturbed it. If you see a horned toad, leave it alone!

1. Rafael's main purpose is to

_____ persuade _____.

entertain   inform   persuade

2. Rafael probably is afraid of horned toads.

likes horned toads
is afraid of horned toads
knows a lot about lizards

3. Rafael would probably agree that strange-looking creatures

should be left alone.

can be helpful
are actually beautiful
should be left alone

Robert's Report

The horned toad is a harmless little creature that is often misunderstood. It may look a little scary with its sharp spines, but it does no harm. The spines are just to protect it from enemies. Don't let its mean glare fool you. The horned toad won't hurt you at all.

4. Robert's main purpose is to

_____ persuade _____.

entertain   inform   persuade

5. Robert probably doesn't judge creatures by looks.

likes only pretty creatures
doesn't judge creatures by looks
thinks all lizards are ugly

6. Robert would probably agree that

looks can fool you.

scary-looking creatures are bad
lizards are not helpful to humans
looks can fool you

 TRY THIS! Think about an insect or other creature that looks a little scary. Do you like the creature or not? Write a paragraph to persuade readers to agree with you.

Harcourt

Name _____

| Skill Reminder | To decode a long word, look for a prefix, a suffix, or a familiar word part. |

▶ Read the newspaper article. Complete the chart by writing *prefix*, *suffix*, or *familiar word part* to indicate a strategy or strategies for figuring out each underlined word. Then write the word's meaning from the phrases in the box.

Talented Students Entertain Crowd

The fourth-grade students from the Cedar Park School put on an extraordinary performance at City Park last evening. Three girls sang together, their voices blending in harmonious tunes. Several students performed their own compositions on guitar and drums. One young man even played the bagpipes. For more than an hour, music resounded throughout the park.

musical instrument made of a bag and several pipes
having pleasing harmony   better than ordinary
music that is composed   echoed with sound

Word	Strategy	Meaning
1. extraordinary	familiar word part, prefix	better than ordinary
2. harmonious	familiar word part, suffix	having pleasing harmony
3. compositions	familiar word part, suffix	music that is composed
4. bagpipes	familiar word parts	musical instrument made of a bag and several pipes
5. resounded	familiar word part, prefix	echoed with sound

Harcourt

▶ **Before you read, fill in the prediction chart by writing what you think will happen. After you read, write what actually happens.**
Possible responses are given.

What I Predict Will Happen	What Actually Happens
Janey will talk Dad into letting her go to the town school.	Dad does not let Janey go to the town school.
Janey will run away from the camp school.	Janey goes inside the camp school.
Janey will let her horned toad loose in school.	Janey uses her toad to test her new teacher.
Janey's teacher will call it a horned lizard.	Her teacher calls it a horned toad.
	Janey feels good about her new teacher and the new school.

▶ **Write a one-sentence summary telling how Miss Peterson gets Janey to change her negative attitude.**

Possible response: Miss Peterson is friendly, quotes Mother Goose, gives

the toad an interesting name, and makes Janey feel part of the class.

_____

Harcourt

Name _____

▶ **Read the definitions. Write the meaning of each underlined word as it is used in each sentence.**

bee: **(a)** a type of insect; **(b)** a gathering of people

board: **(a)** a thin slab of material having a certain purpose, as a chalkboard; **(b)** a group of people who direct something

pens: **(a)** small fenced areas for keeping animals; **(b)** instruments for writing with ink

stories: **(a)** tales; **(b)** floors of a building

yard: **(a)** a measurement of 36 inches; **(b)** the ground next to a building

1. My great-aunt went to school in a building two <u>stories</u> tall.

   floors of a building

2. Her desk was only about a <u>yard</u> away from the teacher's desk.

   a measurement of 36 inches

3. One day a <u>bee</u> flew in through the window and caused a panic.

   a type of insect

4. The teacher had the students read <u>stories</u> about faraway places like Borneo.

   tales

5. Ink and <u>pens</u> were not allowed, so Aunt Margaret wrote with pencil.

   instruments for writing with ink

6. She also liked to write and draw on the <u>board</u>.

   a thin slab of material having a certain purpose, as a chalkboard

7. The school <u>board</u> placed an American flag in every classroom.

   a group of people who direct something

8. Aunt Margaret's class always had a spelling <u>bee</u> on Friday.

   a gathering of people

9. At recess the students played in the grassy <u>yard</u> behind the school.

   the ground next to a building

10. The farmer kept the pigs in <u>pens</u>.

    small fenced areas for keeping animals

SCHOOL-HOME CONNECTION With your child, begin a list of words you hear or see that have more than one meaning. Keep the list in a place where both of you can add to it easily.

Touch a Dream **175**

▶ *Denotation* is the exact or dictionary meaning of a word. *Connotation* is the meaning a word suggests. Read each pair of sentences. Then answer the questions that follow.

When we first moved to the farm, Pa built a small shed for us to live in. Next to our neighbor's beautiful house, it looked like a shack.

1. Which two words denote a *small building*? _____ shed, shack _____

2. Which of the two words you wrote connotes *something that is disliked*? _____ shack _____

3. Does the word *mansion* have a negative or a positive connotation? _____ positive _____

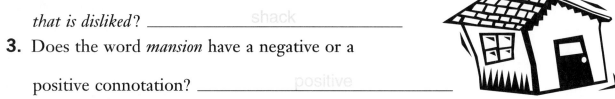

The fabric in this old dress is worn. It looks ragged compared to my other clothes.

4. Which two words denote *shabby*? _____ worn, ragged _____

5. Which of the words you wrote connotes *extremely shabby*? _____ ragged _____

6. Does the word *elegant* have a negative or a positive connotation?

_____ positive _____

This morning when I was washing dishes, I broke my mother's favorite plate. I was very upset when it shattered on the floor.

7. Which two words denote *caused to come apart*? _____ broke, shattered _____

8. Which of the words you wrote connotes *into many pieces*? _____ shattered _____

9. Does the word *mend* have a negative or a positive connotation? _____ positive _____

My grandma was happy when she saw us drive up. She was delighted when she saw that we had brought the dog along, too.

10. Which two words denote *pleased*? _____ happy, delighted _____

11. Which of the words you wrote connotes *extremely pleased*? _____ delighted _____

12. Does the word *miserable* have a negative or a positive connotation?

_____ negative _____

Name _____

▶ **Write the verb from each sentence in the column where it belongs.**

1. The migrant workers picked cotton all week.

2. Later they will help with the berry crop.

3. Some of the workers arrived from up North.

4. Others stayed out West most of the year.

5. A few workers will eventually become landowners.

6. Most will return to the fields next year.

Past-Tense Verbs	Future-Tense Verbs
picked	will help
arrived	will become
stayed	will return

▶ **Complete each sentence with the correct form of the verb in parentheses ( ).**

7. We _____ moved _____ in the middle of the year. (**move—past tense**)

8. In this town, school _____ started _____ very early. (**start—past tense**)

9. We _____ will meet _____ other migrant workers' children.
(**meet—future tense**)

10. As we get to know each other, we _____ will become _____ friends.
(**become—future tense**)

TRY THIS! Think of two action verbs that end in *-ed* in the past tense. On a separate sheet of paper, use each verb in a past-tense sentence and in a future-tense sentence.

Harcourt

Name _____

▶ **Write a Spelling Word to complete each sentence.**

SPELLING WORDS

1. *stepped*
2. *entered*
3. *reaching*
4. *allowing*
5. *argued*
6. *speaking*
7. *reading*
8. *unfolding*
9. *finished*
10. *closing*
11. *hugged*
12. *belonged*

1. Max ___entered___ the classroom.

2. Meanwhile, Bruce and Tia are ___unfolding___ the flag outside.

3. Tran's job this week is ___closing___ the door after the class leaves the room.

4. No one ___argued___ about letting Tran do it.

5. Bob is ___reading___ a funny book.

6. Look! I'm ___reaching___ the top shelf.

7. I feel shy when I'm ___speaking___ to the class.

8. Luz and I ___finished___ first.

9. This puppy ___belonged___ to my neighbor.

10. Carlos has ___stepped___ outside.

11. We ___hugged___ the puppies carefully.

12. All the puppies are ___allowing___ us to be their friends.

Handwriting Tip: Take care to close the letter *d* and don't loop the up and down strokes, or it might look like *cl*. Write the Spelling Words below.

entered

13. stepped ___stepped___   15. argued ___argued___

14. reading ___reading___   16. hugged ___hugged___

Harcourt

Name _____

▶ **Choose words from the lamppost to complete the sentences below.**

culture　　chile　　barbecue　　mesquite　　confetti　/ accordion

Attention All Neighbors!

This Saturday and Sunday we will hold an outdoor

(1) _____barbecue_____ in our neighborhood. The purpose

is to celebrate the **(2)** _____culture_____ of the
Southwest. All kinds of food will be served, including some tacos,

and some hot, spicy **(3)** _____chile_____!
We'll supply everything from the cups and plates to the coals of

(4) _____mesquite_____ wood! Just bring your appetites!

A musician will play the **(5)** _____accordion_____.

Sing along! Throw **(6)** _____confetti_____!

Come celebrate!

▶ **Write the word from the lamppost that completes each analogy.**

7. *Tomato* is to *ketchup* as *spice* is to _____chile_____.

8. *Strum* is to *guitar* as *squeeze* is to _____accordion_____.

9. *Log* is to *wood chips* as *paper* is to _____confetti_____.

10. *Sandwich* is to *picnic* as *hamburger* is to _____barbecue_____.

SCHOOL-HOME CONNECTION With your child, talk about your
favorite family meals, vacations, or traditions. Use at least two of
the Vocabulary Words.

Touch a Dream **179**

Harcourt

▶ **Complete the character map below. Include information about each character.** Possible responses are given.

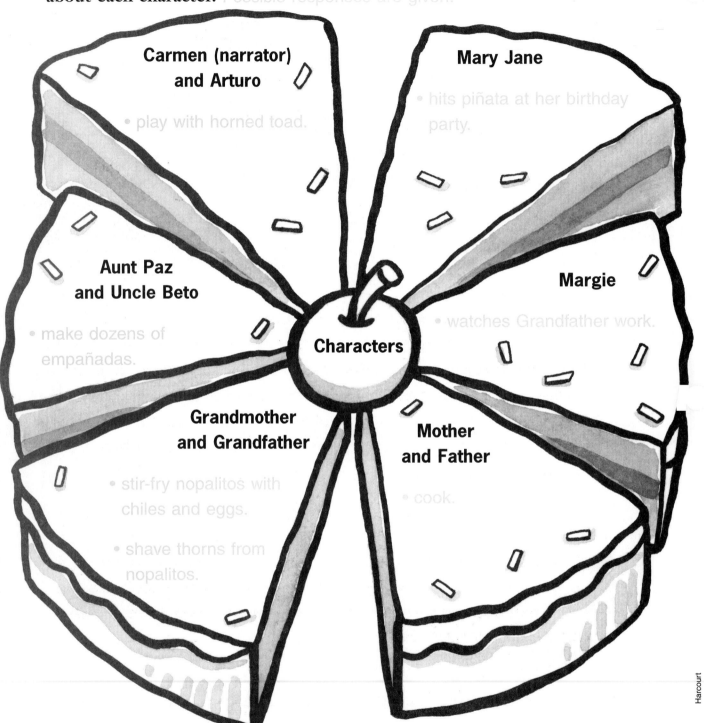

Carmen (narrator) and Arturo
• play with horned toad.

Mary Jane
• hits piñata at her birthday party.

Aunt Paz and Uncle Beto
• make dozens of empanadas.

Characters

Margie
• watches Grandfather work.

Grandmother and Grandfather
• stir-fry nopalitos with chiles and eggs.
• shave thorns from nopalitos.

Mother and Father
• cook.

▶ **How can you tell that Carmen's family is a close one?**

Possible response: They have many family celebrations and frequently work

and play together. They also watch out for and care for one other.

Name _____

▶ **Skim the article below. Then, on the next page, answer
the questions.**

At Home in a Castle

Can you imagine what it was like to live in a castle? Hundreds of years
ago, rich landowners called lords built strong buildings where they and the
people who lived nearby could be safe when enemies attacked. One kind of
castle was called a *motte and bailey* castle. The motte was the tall mound of
earth where a tower was built. The bailey was the courtyard where many
smaller buildings were located.

The Bailey

For protection from enemies, the bailey was surrounded by a *moat*, a
ditch filled with water. A wooden drawbridge could be lowered across the
moat to let people into the bailey. Inside the moat, a fence encircled the
bailey. The buildings and fences were both made of wood. Sometimes
attackers burned them down.

A Community Inside

The bailey was really a small village. There was a stable for housing the
animals. Barracks provided a place for the lord's soldiers to stay. A barn
and storehouses held food and other supplies. There might even be a small
church, a kitchen, and a bakery. Feasts were held in the great hall. The
bailey could be very crowded with servants, workers, and soldiers all going
about their business.

GO ON ⇨

Harcourt

▶ **Now that you have skimmed the article on the preceding page, write the answer to the questions below. Choose from the words or phrases below each line. You may turn back to scan for information when necessary.**

1. From the title and headings, you can tell that this article is about

   _____ life in a castle _____ .

   life in a castle   how to be a knight   life on the frontier

2. To find out what materials were used to build the bailey, the reader should

   look in the section under the heading _____ The Bailey _____ .

   The Bailey   A Community Inside   At Home in a Castle

3. The section "A Community Inside" will probably be about

   _____ activities in the castle _____ .

   what knights ate   how to build walls   activities in the castle

4. A bailey was _____ a courtyard _____ .

   a tall tower   a moat   a courtyard

5. A motte and bailey castle was made of _____ wood _____ .

   stone   wood   bricks

6. A lord was _____ a rich landowner _____ .

   a kind of church   a kind of castle   a rich landowner

7. A moat was _____ a ditch around the bailey _____ .

   the great hall   a drawbridge   a ditch around the bailey

8. Soldiers stayed in the _____ barracks _____ .

   great hall   motte   barracks

9. Feasts were held in the _____ great hall _____ .

   tower   great hall   storehouses

10. The bailey was crowded with _____ soldiers and workers _____ .

    lords and ladies   knights and bakers   soldiers and workers

Harcourt

Name _____

▶ **Complete the chart with the correct form of each verb.**

Verb	Present	Past	Past with Helping Verb
1. be	am, is, are	was, were	(have, has, had) been
2. go	go, goes	went	(have, has, had) gone
3. think	think, thinks	thought	(have, has, had) thought
4. know	know, knows	knew	(have, has, had) known
5. wear	wear, wears	wore	(have, has, had) worn

▶ **Complete each sentence with the correct past-tense or helping-verb form of the verb in parentheses ( ).**

6. Grandma _____wore_____ a colorful apron. **(wear)**

7. She _____broke_____ four eggs into a bowl. **(break)**

8. Then she _____threw_____ the shells in the trash. **(throw)**

9. Outside, the day had _____begun_____. **(begin)**

10. Grandpa had _____brought_____ in the newspaper. **(bring)**

TRY THIS! Choose two verbs from the chart. Write two sentences for each verb. In the first sentence, use the past-tense form. In the second sentence, use the past with a helping verb.

Harcourt

▶ **Write the Spelling Word that rhymes with each word below.**

1. home _____ comb

2. out _____ doubt

3. ham _____ lamb

4. hums _____ crumbs

5. missile _____ whistle

6. strum _____ thumb

▶ **Unscramble the underlined letters. Write the correct Spelling Words on the lines.**

7. I <u>fento</u> think about painting. _____ often

8. I mix paints to <u>tenfos</u> colors. _____ soften

9. I <u>staenf</u> my mind on the scene I want to paint. _____ fasten

10. I sing while I paint, but don't let anyone <u>nestil</u>. _____ listen

11. My favorite painting shows the tower of an old <u>stacel</u>. _____ castle

12. I <u>mebcdli</u> up the tower. _____ climbed

SPELLING WORDS
1. lamb
2. often
3. castle
4. listen
5. comb
6. climbed
7. fasten
8. crumbs
9. soften
10. thumb
11. doubt
12. whistle

Handwriting Tip: Use an overcurve joining stroke in writing *m*, so that it doesn't look like *n*. Write the Spelling Words below. ⟋m

13. lamb _____ lamb **15.** climbed _____ climbed

14. comb _____ comb **16.** thumb _____ thumb

SCHOOL-HOME CONNECTION With your child, use the first six Spelling Words in three sentences. Help your child use two words in each sentence.

▶ **Write the word from the pots that matches each clue.**

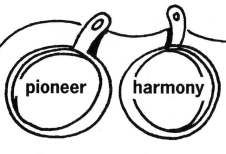 

pioneer harmony fertile arbor possibilities

1. things that may happen _____ possibilities

2. musical notes sung together _____ harmony

3. a shelter shaded by
   vines or branches _____ arbor

4. able to produce a lot _____ fertile

5. an early settler _____ pioneer

▶ **Write the Vocabulary Word that answers each riddle.**

6. I sound nice in a song.
   What am I? _____ harmony

7. I traveled to live on unsettled
   land. Who am I? _____ pioneer

8. With me, anything may
   happen. What am I? _____ possibilities

9. I'm a shelter covered with
   vines. What am I? _____ arbor

10. My kind of soil grows many
    crops. What kind of soil am I? _____ fertile

TRY THIS! Imagine that you are a pioneer on another planet. Describe what you see
and hear and how you live. Use at least two Vocabulary Words.

Harcourt

Touch a Dream **185**

Name _____

Skill Reminder Use encyclopedias, dictionaries, atlases, and globes to help you find information.

▶ Help Molly prepare a report about Oklahoma. Beside each question, write where she should look for the information she needs. Choose from the words in the box.

| encyclopedia | dictionary | atlas | globe |

1. What states border on Oklahoma? _____ atlas, globe, or encyclopedia

2. When did Oklahoma become a state? _____ encyclopedia

3. How far is it from my hometown to Oklahoma City? _____ atlas

4. What crops are grown in Oklahoma? _____ encyclopedia

5. What place is on the exact opposite side of Earth from Oklahoma? _____ globe

6. Why is Oklahoma called "The Sooner State"? _____ encyclopedia

7. How is the word *drought* pronounced? _____ dictionary

8. Which major highways pass through Tulsa, Oklahoma? _____ atlas

9. What are some important dates in Oklahoma's history? _____ encyclopedia

10. Does Oklahoma have any lakes and rivers? _____ atlas or encyclopedia

TRY THIS! Plan a report about your state. Make a list of the information you need and where you would find it.

Harcourt

Name _____

Skill Reminder   A generalization is a conclusion based on information the writer gives.

▶ Read this passage from a diary that Lizzie wrote about her family's experience as homesteaders. Then write *valid* or *invalid* beside each generalization.

I'll never forget how blue and bright that Oklahoma sky was when I was a child! The first year that our family lived on our homestead in the Oklahoma Territory, it hardly rained at all. The soil felt like stone, and it was hard work to plow it and plant crops. For weeks we watched the sky, hoping for rain to water the seeds and make them grow. Those were hard times. We didn't get a crop that first year, so we had nothing to sell so we could buy supplies. It was a good thing that Mother planted a patch of vegetables. Her garden was near our well, so we were able to water it. The beans and peas and potatoes she raised were enough to keep the family fed. Our second year was much better. Father raised a good crop, and we children even got new pairs of shoes!

Generalization	Valid or Invalid
1. It never rains in Oklahoma.	invalid
2. Soil becomes hard when it is very dry.	valid
3. Homesteaders had no shoes.	invalid
4. Homesteaders needed rain for their crops.	valid
5. Dry years made for hard times for homesteaders.	valid
6. All homesteaders planted vegetable gardens.	invalid
7. Vegetable gardens helped keep some homesteaders from being hungry.	valid
8. It is always hot in Oklahoma.	invalid
9. All homesteaders were happy.	invalid
10. Weather was important to homesteaders.	valid

Harcourt

▶ **Complete the cause-and-effect fishbone.**
Possible responses are given.

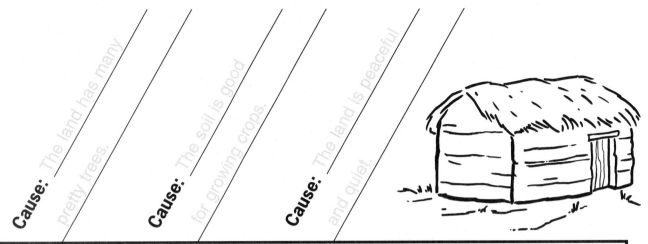

Cause: The land has many pretty trees.

Cause: The soil is good for growing crops.

Cause: The land is peaceful and quiet.

Effect: The narrator claims land in the Oklahoma Territory.

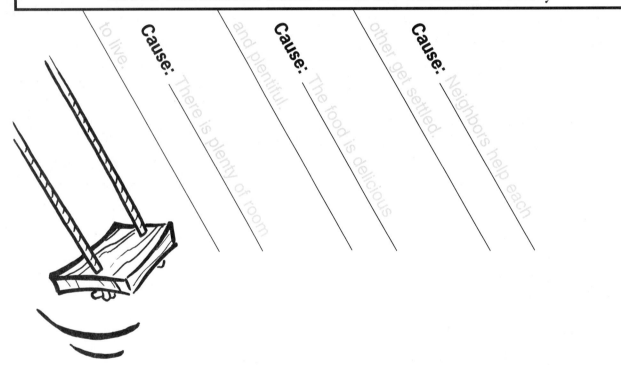

Cause: There is plenty of room to live.

Cause: The food is delicious and plentiful.

Cause: Neighbors help each other get settled.

▶ **Write a one-sentence summary of the whole selection.**

Possible response: The narrator is a pioneer woman who settles in a land

that has wide-open spaces, harsh winters, peace and quiet, fertile fields for

growing crops, sod huts and log cabins, friendly neighbors, and possibilities

for fulfilling dreams.

Name _____

▶ **Read the words and their meanings. In each sentence, use context clues to help you decide what the underlined word means in that sentence. Then write that meaning of the word.**

	Meaning 1	**Meaning 2**	**Meaning 3**
crop:	a product grown on a farm	trim the edges	a short haircut
draft:	related to pulling heavy loads	select for a job	a current of air
raise:	grow	set up or build	an increase in pay
stable:	a building for animals	not easy to shake or move	not changing
smart:	intelligent	in style	feel a sharp sting

1. I cut my finger on the edge of one of the photos, and did that ever <u>smart</u>!

    feel a sharp sting

2. I had to <u>crop</u> some of the photos so they would fit in my album.

    trim the edges

3. These pictures show the garden where we <u>raise</u> vegetables.

    grow

4. This photo shows a field of corn, our best <u>crop</u>.

    a product grown on a farm

5. We use horses as <u>draft</u> animals to pull loaded wagons.

    used for pulling heavy loads

6. Our biggest horse, Jeb, helped <u>raise</u> the walls of our new house by pulling the boards into place.

    set up or build

7. We nailed the boards together so our walls would be <u>stable</u> when strong winds blow.

    not easy to shake or move

8. Jeb is so <u>smart</u> that he seems to know what to do before we tell him.

    intelligent

TRY THIS! Look in a dictionary and find an unfamiliar word that has more than one meaning. Write sentences using each meaning of the word.

Harcourt

Name _____

▶ **Read each sentence. Choose the answer that best tells the meaning of the underlined word as it is used in the sentence. Mark the letter of that answer.**

1 I read an exciting <u>novel</u> about pioneer life.

  Ⓐ new or unusual

  Ⓑ sports event

  Ⓒ a long piece of fiction

  Ⓓ type of farm

2 The pioneers built their houses in a <u>novel</u> way, using blocks of earth called sod.

  Ⓕ new or unusual

  Ⓖ brick

  Ⓗ a long piece of fiction

  Ⓙ modern

3 A pioneer would build a <u>shed</u> to store equipment or food.

  Ⓐ to send forth

  Ⓑ to cast off

  Ⓒ a small, low building

  Ⓓ "she would"

4 Sometimes a snowstorm would <u>strand</u> a family on the prairie for weeks.

  Ⓕ a thread twisted into a rope

  Ⓖ to leave helpless

  Ⓗ a beach or shore

  Ⓙ to run a ship onto the shore

5 Grasshoppers, weevils, and <u>flies</u> were pests on the farms.

  Ⓐ kind of insect

  Ⓑ runs away

  Ⓒ moves quickly

  Ⓓ travels through the air

6 Often a hired <u>hand</u> became more like a family member than just a helper.

  Ⓕ body part at the end of the arm

  Ⓖ a round of clapping

  Ⓗ worker

  Ⓙ a pointer on a clock

7 Trees were so rare on the plains that they were <u>points</u> of interest.

  Ⓐ sharp tips

  Ⓑ brings attention with a stick or a finger

  Ⓒ certain places

  Ⓓ a strip of land that extends into a body of water

Name _____

▶ **Write the word that means the same as the underlined word.**

1. I like my <u>flapjacks</u> with butter and syrup.

Flapjacks are probably _____pancakes_____.

cookies　　　　　**pancakes**　　　　　**eggrolls**

2. Mom said she would <u>fix</u> dinner.

Fix probably means _____prepare_____.

fasten　　　　　**prepare**　　　　　**repair**

3. Our breakfast of <u>grits</u> warmed us as we ventured out in the snow.

Grits are probably _____hot cereal_____.

hot cereal　　　　　**eggs**　　　　　**toast**

4. Jimmy loved to fish for <u>crawdads</u>.

Crawdads are probably _____crayfish_____.

fathers　　　　　**squirrels**　　　　　**crayfish**

5. The <u>cane</u> crop produced a lot of sugar this year.

Cane is probably a _____sugar plant_____.

stick for walking　　　**sugar plant**　　　**candy**

6. We ground the <u>goobers</u> until we had peanut butter.

Goobers are probably _____peanuts_____.

leaves　　　　　**raisins**　　　　　**peanuts**

7. Mom and I sat on the front <u>stoop</u> and watched our neighbors

walking past. *Stoop* probably means _____porch_____.

shed　　　　　**sidewalk**　　　　　**porch**

8. Jesse bought a new <u>skillet</u> for cooking eggs.

A *skillet* is probably _____a frying pan_____.

a teapot　　　**something to learn**　　　**a frying pan**

TRY THIS! Ask your family, friends, and teacher about words that are unique to where you live. Keep a running list of these regional words.

Name _____

▶ **Write the contraction for each word pair.**

1. she is _____ she's

2. have not _____ haven't

3. would not _____ wouldn't

4. is not _____ isn't

5. I have _____ I've

6. he had _____ he'd

7. it is _____ it's

8. do not _____ don't

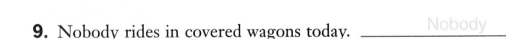

▶ **Write the negative from each sentence.**

9. Nobody rides in covered wagons today. _____ Nobody

10. Wagons were never a great way to travel. _____ never

▶ **Rewrite each sentence. Get rid of double negatives. Use the correct pronoun or contraction.**

11. You never wanted to be no pioneer.

You never wanted to be a pioneer.

12. Your sure its too hard a life?

You're sure it's too hard a life?

TRY THIS!

Use each word pair in a sentence.
  its/it's   *their/they're*
Use each word in a sentence.
  nobody   *never*

Harcourt

Name _____

▶ **Write the contraction for each of the underlined words.**

1. Life <u>was not</u> easy for pioneers.   wasn't

2. They <u>did not</u> have any luxuries.   didn't

3. <u>I would</u> miss a microwave oven.   I'd

4. <u>You would</u> miss canned food.   You'd

5. We <u>have not</u> had to chop wood.   haven't

6. Mom says <u>she would</u> like to
   try living the life of a pioneer.   she'd

7. Who <u>would not</u> like to?   wouldn't

8. <u>I have</u> read that tourists can
   take trips in covered wagons.   I've

9. Now <u>we have</u> written to
   several travel agencies.   we've

10. Here are the pamphlets
    <u>they have</u> sent us.   they've

11. One company still
    <u>has not</u> replied.   hasn't

12. After <u>you have</u> read
    this brochure, tell me
    what you think of it.   you've

SPELLING WORDS

1. *hasn't*
2. *I've*
3. *I'd*
4. *we've*
5. *wouldn't*
6. *you'd*
7. *haven't*
8. *wasn't*
9. *they've*
10. *you've*
11. *she'd*
12. *didn't*

Handwriting Tip: When you write a contraction, do not connect the letter before the apostrophe to the letter after the apostrophe. Write the Spelling Words below.

hasn't

13. hasn't _____   15. they've _____

14. haven't _____   16. she'd _____

Harcourt

Name _____

▶ **Write the word below that completes each sentence.**

bellowing   softhearted   ration   tragedy   fateful   gadgets

Many tall tales tell of legendary characters who are big both in size and in deeds. Somehow though, we tend to think of giants as unpleasant. Remember the giant in "Jack and the Beanstalk"? Was he kind and **(1)** _____ softhearted _____, or was he scary? If the giant had plenty of food, do you think he would share it freely with others or **(2)** _____ ration _____ it in very small amounts? Can you imagine what it would sound like to hear the giant

(3) _____ bellowing _____ for his pet? Can you picture the size of his household **(4)** _____ gadgets _____, such as his can opener or nutcracker? It is a **(5)** _____ tragedy _____ that because of one mean giant, other giants are thought of in the same way. Paul Bunyan was kind and **(6)** _____ softhearted _____. You would never hear him

(7) _____ bellowing _____ at his pet ox unless he thought Babe was lost. He was the best logger ever. It was a **(8)** _____ fateful _____ day when Paul Bunyan decided to stop working.

▶ **Write the Vocabulary Word that means the *opposite* of each word below.**

9. comedy _____ tragedy _____

10. strict _____ softhearted _____

11. whispering _____ bellowing _____

12. foreboding _____ fateful _____

TRY THIS! Make up your own story about something unusual that Paul Bunyan and Babe did. Use at least two Vocabulary Words.

Name _____

Paul Bunyan and
Babe the Blue Ox

Words with More
Than One Meaning

Art

Skill Reminder Some words have more than one meaning. Use context clues to help you figure out the word's meaning in the sentence.

▶ Write the meaning that each underlined word has. Choose from the meanings in the box.

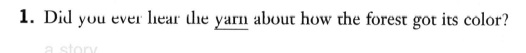

bit: (a) a tiny amount; **(b)** the metal part of a bridle that fits in a horse's mouth
bored: (a) made weary by being dull; **(b)** made a hole through
bright: (a) clever; **(b)** glowing with color or light
plain: (a) not decorated or fancy; **(b)** a level area of land
sport: (a) a game or contest; **(b)** to wear or display
stir: (a) excitement or great interest; **(b)** to move around with a circular motion
yarn: (a) a story; **(b)** a type of string used in knitting and weaving

1. Did you ever hear the <u>yarn</u> about how the forest got its color?

a story _____

2. Long ago, everything in the forest was <u>plain</u> black and white and gray, just like in an old movie. not decorated or fancy _____

3. Jiggs Jiggerson, who was a <u>bright</u> young lad, put his brain to work on the problem. clever _____

4. First he <u>bored</u> a hole in the sky and drained out some blue.

made a hole through _____

5. Then Jiggs sliced off a <u>bit</u> of yellow from the sun. a tiny amount _____

6. He began to <u>stir</u> the blue and yellow together, and got green.

to move around with a circular motion _____

7. Jiggs got to work with his paintbrush, and soon every tree in the forest could <u>sport</u> pretty green leaves. to wear or display _____

TRY THIS! Use some underlined words on this page to write your own tall tale.

Harcourt

Touch a Dream **195**

▶ **Before you read the story and as you read, fill in the prediction chart by writing what you think will happen. After you read, write what actually happens.** Possible responses are given.

What I Predict Will Happen	What Actually Happens
Paul's crew will ask Paul to send Babe away.	Paul's crew takes a liking to Babe.
The giant bees will chase away the giant mosquitoes.	The bees and mosquitoes intermarry and produce offspring.
The thousands of oxen will help Babe haul lumber.	The oxen are involved in a tragic accident.

▶ **Write a one-sentence summary describing what Paul relies on Babe for through the years.**

Possible response: Paul relies on Babe to haul lumber, and to be a pet

and close companion.

_____

Harcourt

Name _____

▶ **Read the story beginning. Then write *yes* or *no* after each statement to indicate whether a reader could correctly make that inference.**

I was standing in my cabin, looking out the window at the beautiful stack of firewood I'd just finished chopping, when I saw something that made my hair stand on end. "Jackie! Frankie! Tess!" I yelled to my kids. "Will you look at that!" The kids came running to the window and looked out.

"Bees, Papa!" cried Tess.

"The biggest bees I ever saw!" shouted Jackie.

"Yes," I cried, "and they're trying to build a hive in my pile of firewood!" Quick as a wink, we ran outside, yelling, "Scram, you bees!" One bee had already picked up my ax and was trying to chop a hole in a big log for a doorway. You won't believe what happened next.

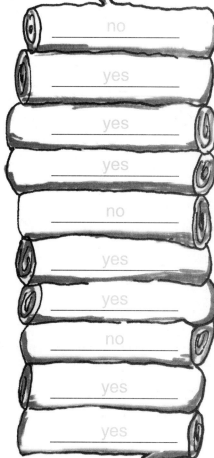

1. This is a true story. _____ no

2. The person telling the story is a father. _____ yes

3. An ax is a tool for chopping firewood. _____ yes

4. The storyteller is proud of his stack of firewood. _____ yes

5. Only four people live in the cabin. _____ no

6. The storyteller has at least three children. _____ yes

7. The storyteller burns wood. _____ yes

8. The children can chop firewood. _____ no

9. The storyteller was very surprised by the bees. _____ yes

10. The storyteller doesn't want bees in his firewood. _____ yes

TRY THIS! Reread a passage from one of your favorite stories. Make a list of the inferences you can make from the passage.

Harcourt

▶ **Underline the verb. Circle the adverb that describes it.
Then tell whether the adverb tells *where, when,* or *how.***

1. The huge ox rushed over.   _where_

2. He quickly drank the whole lake.   _how_

3. The loggers shouted angrily.   _how_

4. They never saw such a thirsty beast. _when_

5. A thousand fish flopped nearby.   _where_

6. Now Babe felt content.   _when_

7. He lay down with a grunt.   _where_

8. Later, the loggers heard a roar.   _when_

9. Dropping their axes, they ran fast.   _how_

10. The blue ox snored peacefully.   _how_

▶ **Rewrite each sentence. Add an adverb that gives the information
in parentheses ( ).**
Responses will vary; possible responses are given.

11. Babe took a nap. **(when)** _Babe took a nap today._

12. The loggers rested. **(where)** _The loggers rested upstairs._

Harcourt

SCHOOL-HOME CONNECTION Look at some family photographs
with your child. Then have your child write captions for several of the
photographs, using an adverb in each caption. Here are some examples:
Grandma smiles happily.   *Aunt Sara always brings pie.*

Name _____

▶ Write two Spelling Words to complete each sentence. Use a pair of homophones in each sentence.

1.–2. I'll give you _____some_____ numbers to add,

and you can tell us the _____sum_____.

3.–4. Do you want to hear the _____tale_____ of

a bear with a long, bushy _____tail_____?

5.–6. As we stood on the _____plains_____, we saw

two _____planes_____ flying overhead.

7.–8. The wind _____blew_____ so hard that our

_____blue_____ tent nearly collapsed.

9.–10. Please _____close_____ the door to the

_____clothes_____ closet.

11.–12. Clearly, we'll have no _____peace_____

until we give the dog a _____piece_____
of our meat.

SPELLING WORDS
1. some
2. sum
3. tale
4. plains
5. close
6. blew
7. piece
8. clothes
9. tail
10. planes
11. blue
12. peace

Handwriting Tip: Make sure the letter *l* touches the top writing line. Otherwise, it might look like an *e*. Write the Spelling Words below.

tale

13. plains _____plains_____   **15.** planes _____planes_____

14. blew _____blew_____   **16.** blue _____blue_____

Harcourt

▶ **Write the word from the boat that matches each clue. Some words will be used twice. The message in the oar tells you what nationality TJ's mother is.**

hysterically	overwhelm	interpreter	appetizing
equivalent	irrigation	occasionally	

1. equal _e_ _q_ _u_ _i_ _v_ _a_ _l_ _e_ _n_ _t_

2. sometimes _o_ _c_ _c_ _a_ _s_ _i_ _o_ _n_ _a_ _l_ _l_ _y_

3. overpower _o_ _v_ _e_ _r_ _w_ _h_ _e_ _l_ _m_

4. system for watering _i_ _r_ _r_ _i_ _g_ _a_ _t_ _i_ _o_ _n_

5. translator _i_ _n_ _t_ _e_ _r_ _p_ _r_ _e_ _t_ _e_ _r_

6. very tasty _a_ _p_ _p_ _e_ _t_ _i_ _z_ _i_ _n_ _g_

7. rush at and crush _o_ _v_ _e_ _r_ _w_ _h_ _e_ _l_ _m_

8. with wild emotion _h_ _y_ _s_ _t_ _e_ _r_ _i_ _c_ _a_ _l_ _l_ _y_

9. once in a while _o_ _c_ _c_ _a_ _s_ _i_ _o_ _n_ _a_ _l_ _l_ _y_

10. the same as _e_ _q_ _u_ _i_ _v_ _a_ _l_ _e_ _n_ _t_

SCHOOL-HOME CONNECTION With your child, talk about the countries your family's relatives and ancestors came from. Tell about the trips those people made to come to the United States. Use at least three Vocabulary Words.

Harcourt

Name _____

Skill Reminder Use context clues to help you figure out what an unfamiliar word means.

▶ Read the sentences. Use context clues to help you figure out what each underlined word means. Then write each underlined word beside its meaning listed below.

The eel is not a snake, but it is so long and <u>slender</u> that it looks a little like one. <u>Naturalists</u> study eels to learn more about their life cycle.

Crocodiles like warm weather, so they live in <u>tropical</u> areas. They <u>inhabit</u> places where there is shallow water. Crocodiles are <u>aggressive</u> animals and may attack large animals or people. Be careful not to <u>agitate</u> a crocodile!

Some water buffalo are no longer wild animals and have been <u>domesticated</u> for use as farm animals. They are <u>brawny</u> animals and can pull a plow in deep mud. In fact, they <u>revel</u> in wallowing in mud! The milk of the water buffalo is healthful and <u>nourishing</u>.

1. quick to attack _____ aggressive

2. to enjoy very much _____ revel

3. thin _____ slender

4. to live in a place _____ inhabit

5. describing something that keeps someone healthy _____ nourishing

6. scientists who study nature _____ naturalists

7. strong _____ brawny

8. to disturb or excite _____ agitate

9. tamed _____ domesticated

10. located in the hot, wet part of the Earth near the equator _____ tropical

SCHOOL-HOME CONNECTION With your child, find a magazine article. Help your child use context clues to find the meanings of unfamiliar words.

Harcourt

Name _____

▶ **Fill in the first two columns of the K-W-L chart. Then use
information from the story to fill in the last column.**
Possible responses are given.

K	W	L
What I Know	**What I Want to Know**	**What I Learned**
Vietnam is a faraway country in Asia.	What happens when TJ visits his relatives in Vietnam?	TJ notices there are no appliances such as stoves or refrigerators. TJ sees people traveling by bicycle, carrying large loads. TJ tries to plow a field with oxen because there are no tractors. TJ finds out people travel on the river by canoe.

▶ **Think about all the things TJ experiences in Vietnam. List five ways that
life in Vietnam is different from life in America.** Possible responses
are given.

1. Vietnamese farmers use water-buffalo carts instead of tractors.

2. A Vietnamese menu includes grilled sparrows and eel soup.

3. The Vietnamese find ways to stay cool without air-conditioning.

4. The people speak Vietnamese instead of English.

5. People cook on dirt floors in fireplaces with no chimneys.

Harcourt

▶ **Study the map, graph, and diagram. Then answer the questions about each.**

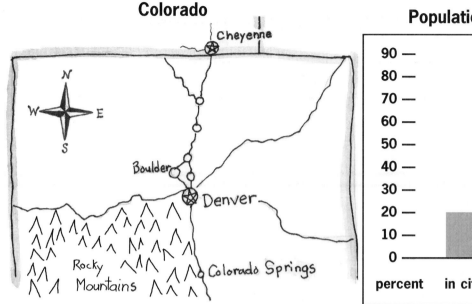

Colorado

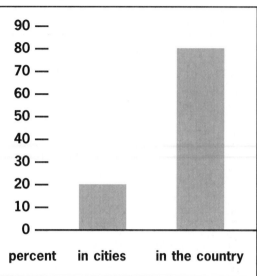

Population of Vietnam

1. In which direction would you travel to go from Denver to Colorado Springs? _____ south

2. What mountain range is found in Colorado? _____ the Rocky Mountains

3. What percentage of Vietnam's people live in cities? _____ 20 percent

4. What percentage of Vietnam's people live in the country? _____ 80 percent

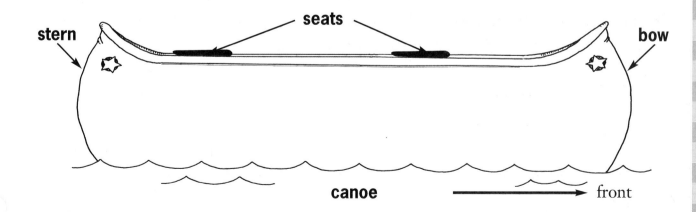

5. What is the front part of the canoe called? _____ bow

Harcourt

Name _____

▶ **Study the table and time line. Then answer the questions.**

	Vietnam	United States
Farm Products	rice, cassava, sweet potatoes, sugarcane, coffee, cotton	corn, wheat, cotton, soybeans, etc.
Languages	Vietnamese, Chinese, English, Khmer	English, Spanish, etc.
Capital	Hanoi	Washington, D.C.
Population	about 74,000,000	about 266,000,000

1. Does Vietnam or the United States have a

   larger population? _____ United States _____

2. Which farm product is grown in both countries? _____ cotton _____

3. Which language is spoken in both countries? _____ English _____

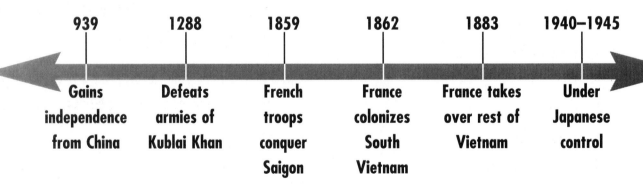

939	1288	1859	1862	1883	1940–1945
Gains independence from China	Defeats armies of Kublai Khan	French troops conquer Saigon	France colonizes South Vietnam	France takes over rest of Vietnam	Under Japanese control

4. In what year did Vietnam gain independence from China? _____ 939 _____

5. What country controlled Vietnam after France? _____ Japan _____

TRY THIS! Think about some school events of the past year, such as special activities and celebrations. Make a time line to show these important events.

Harcourt

Name _____

▶ **Study the table and graph. Then choose the answer that best completes each sentence, and mark the letter of that answer.**

Type of Animal in Vietnam	Examples
Large Mammals	elephants, deer, bears, tigers, leopards
Smaller Mammals	monkeys, squirrels, otters
Reptiles	crocodiles, snakes, lizards

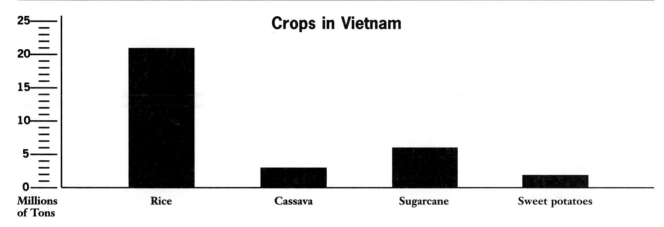

Crops in Vietnam

Millions of Tons

Rice   Cassava   Sugarcane   Sweet potatoes

1 A reptile *not* found in Vietnam is the _____.

   A crocodile

   B alligator

   C snake

   D lizard

2 Vietnam's largest main crop is _____.

   F rice

   G cassava

   H sugarcane

   J sweet potatoes

3 Vietnam grew 6 million tons of _____.

   A rice

   B cassava

   C sugarcane

   D sweet potatoes

4 A map would be best for showing _____.

   F highways and rivers

   G dates when different rulers were in power

   H amounts of rainfall in different years

   J the parts of a plow

5 The best graphic source for showing the design of a helicopter is a _____.

   A map

   B time line

   C graph

   D diagram

Answers
1 Ⓐ Ⓑ Ⓒ Ⓓ
2 Ⓕ Ⓖ Ⓗ Ⓙ
3 Ⓐ Ⓑ Ⓒ Ⓓ
4 Ⓕ Ⓖ Ⓗ Ⓙ
5 Ⓐ Ⓑ Ⓒ Ⓓ

Harcourt

Name _____

Two Lands,
One Heart

Grammar:
Comparing
with Adverbs

▶ **Rewrite each sentence, using the correct form of the adverb in parentheses ( ).**

1. Does rice grow **(taller, tallest)** than corn? Does rice grow taller than corn? _____

_____

2. The ox pulls the **(harder, hardest)** of all the beasts of burden. The ox pulls

the hardest of all the beasts of burden. _____

3. A buffalo plows **(more quickly, most quickly)** than a cow. A buffalo plows

more quickly than a cow. _____

4. The tail of the ox wags **(more jerkily, most jerkily)** of all. The tail of the

ox wags most jerkily of all. _____

5. Do oxen live **(longer, longest)** than buffalo do? Do oxen live longer than

buffalo do? _____

▶ **Complete each sentence with the correct form of the adverb in parentheses ( ).**

6. The van bumped _____ more wildly _____
   than a covered wagon. **(wildly)**

7. It traveled the _____ fastest _____
   of all the vehicles on the road. **(fast)**

8. The road itself wound _____ higher _____
   than the clouds. **(high)**

9. Road crews worked _____ more frequently _____
   in winter than during the monsoon season. **(frequently)**

10. Of all the road's obstacles, the potholes slowed us

    _____ most forcefully _____. **(forcefully)**

Harcourt

▶ **Write the Spelling Word that matches each clue.**

1. They've all joined a group. _____ members

2. It's the opposite of *deep*. _____ shallow

3. It "makes perfect." _____ practice

4. It's an evening meal. _____ dinner

5. Use this word instead of
   imagine. _____ suppose

6. It may be difficult, but you
   can solve it. _____ problem

7. Part of this plant is used to
   make clothes. _____ cotton

8. If you refuse to change
   your mind, people may
   call you this. _____ stubborn

9. It is another word for *thing*. _____ object

10. It's a shiny metal. _____ silver

11. It can protect you from
    bad weather or danger. _____ shelter

12. When you leave something
    out, you often use this word. _____ except

SPELLING WORDS
1. practice
2. members
3. dinner
4. suppose
5. except
6. problem
7. shallow
8. stubborn
9. silver
10. cotton
11. object
12. shelter

Handwriting Tip: Leave enough space between
double letters so they will be easy to read. Write the
Spelling Words below.

cotton

13. suppose _____ suppose   15. cotton _____ cotton

14. stubborn _____ stubborn   16. shallow _____ shallow

SCHOOL-HOME CONNECTION With your child, think of
other words that have double letters. Then find words that
they rhyme with.

Harcourt

Name _____

▶ Write the word from the box that best goes with each pair.
One word will be used twice.

carnivorous	boggiest	chemicals	dissolve
accidentally	fertilizer	victim	

1. melt
liquid

_____dissolve_____

2. grow
plants

_____fertilizer_____

3. meat-eating
hungry

_____carnivorous_____

4. intentionally
unplanned

_____accidentally_____

5. swampy
thickest

_____boggiest_____

6. not on purpose
unexpectedly

_____accidentally_____

7. injured
harmed

_____victim_____

8. scientist
substances

_____chemicals_____

▶ Write the Vocabulary Word from the box above that
means the *opposite* of each term below.

9. vegetable-eating _____carnivorous_____

10. freeze _____dissolve_____

11. attacker _____victim_____

12. intentionally _____accidentally_____

TRY THIS! Imagine that you are a plant or an animal. Write sentences that tell what
you do to survive the dangers where you live. Use some Vocabulary Words.

Harcourt

Name _____

Skill Reminder Use graphs, maps, time lines, tables, and diagrams to help you find information quickly.

▶ Six students planted seeds in flowerpots. Use the graph to see how many of each student's seeds sprouted. Then answer the questions.

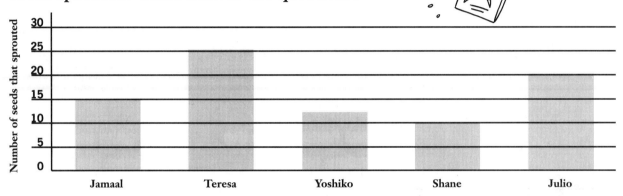

Number of seeds that sprouted

Jamaal   Teresa   Yoshiko   Shane   Julio

1. Which student has about 12 seeds that sprouted? _____Yoshiko_____

2. Which student has more sprouted seeds than Julio? _____Teresa_____

3. How many more of Teresa's seeds sprouted than Shane's? _____15_____

4. If Julio and Jamaal put their sprouted seeds together, how many would

   they have? _____35_____

5. If Yoshiko gave five of her sprouted seeds to Shane, how many would

   Shane have? _____15_____

6. If Teresa gave three of her sprouted seeds to each of the other students,

   which student would have the most? _____Julio_____

7. Would you use a map or a time line to show where different wildflowers

   grow in your state? _____a map_____

8. Would you use a table or a diagram to show the names of different parts of

   a sunflower? _____a diagram_____

TRY THIS! Make a graph to show how many desks, tables, chalkboards, computers, or other items are in your classroom.

Name _____

▶ **Before you read, complete the second column of the SQ3R chart. Complete the third column during and after reading.**
Possible responses are given.

Survey (page, description)	Question	Read, Recite, Review (answer)
page 600 Caption that starts, "There are over 200 different kinds of bladderworts."	What is a bladderwort?	a plant in a pond or river, with bubbles on its stems that catch bugs
page 603 Paragraph that ends, "I sent away for some sundew seeds of my own."	What happens to the sundew seeds?	They grow into baby sun dews but later die after fertilizer gets into their water.
page 605 Paragraph that starts, "I gave up on sundews after that, but I did grow a Venus flytrap."	What is a Venus flytrap?	a plant with tiny trigger hairs that catch flies
page 608 Paragraph that starts, "The next plant I got was a cobra lily."	Why is it called a cobra lily?	Its leaves look like cobras.
page 609 Paragraph that starts, "So I went—all the way to Malaysia."	What was found in Malaysia?	hundreds of pitcher plants

▶ **Write a one-sentence summary of the whole selection.**

Possible response: There are many different plants of all shapes and sizes

that are able to catch flies and other bugs.

Name _____

▶ **Read Marcus's report on strange plants. Then write each underlined word in the group where it belongs.**

Everybody knows that some animals can do tricks, but there are many plants that do surprising things, too. For one thing, not all plants grow in the ground. Molds live on other plants or even on bread or cheese. Moss can live on a rock or a tree. Lichen grows on rocks, too. Ivy is a plant that can climb up a tree or a wall. Honeysuckle and grapevines also climb. Did you know that there are even plants that look like other things? Stone plants are brown and look like desert rocks. The cushion plant of New Zealand looks like a white wool pillow. The traveler's palm tree looks like a peacock's fanned-out tail, and the rain tree looks like a huge umbrella!

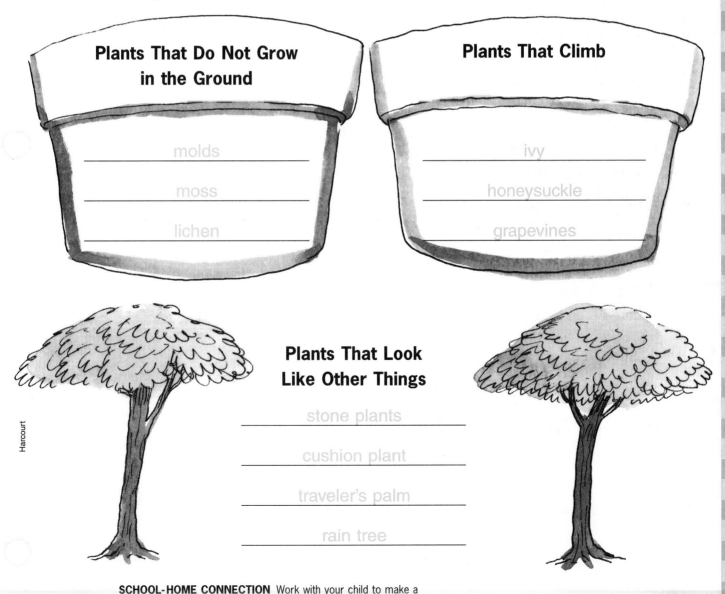

Plants That Do Not Grow in the Ground

molds

moss

lichen

Plants That Climb

ivy

honeysuckle

grapevines

Plants That Look Like Other Things

stone plants

cushion plant

traveler's palm

rain tree

Harcourt

SCHOOL-HOME CONNECTION Work with your child to make a list of fun things to do. Then ask your child to sort the suggestions in different ways, such as "Things to Do Indoors" and "Things to Do Outdoors" or "Things to Do Alone" and "Things to Do Together."

▶ **Underline the preposition. Circle the object of the preposition.**

1. The fly trap grew tall in its tiny pot.

2. It leaned into the sunshine.

3. For a while, it rested quietly.

4. A small fly buzzed over the plant.

5. After a few minutes, the trap snapped.

6. The buzzing of the small insect stopped.

▶ **Use a preposition from the box to complete each sentence. Use each word only once. Use capital letters when necessary.**

across	with	from	into	before	of

7. _____Before_____ noon, the fly trap ate seven bugs.

8. They fell _____into_____ its trap and dissolved.

9. The leaves were armed _____with_____ trigger hairs.

10. The tiniest insects were safe _____from_____ the trap.

11. They walked _____across_____ the hairs safely.

12. Many _____of_____ the fly traps' habitats have been destroyed.

TRY THIS! Choose three of the prepositions from the box above. Use each of them in a separate sentence about plants.

Harcourt

▶ **Unscramble the underlined words. Write the correct Spelling Words on the lines.**

SPELLING WORDS

1. *major*
2. *cedar*
3. *spiders*
4. *locate*
5. *ruler*
6. *motive*
7. *raven*
8. *pilot*
9. *silent*
10. *super*
11. *paper*
12. *native*

1. We want to <u>olecat</u> unusual plants.   locate

2. Venus flytraps are <u>tivena</u> to marshy areas in the southeast.   native

3. Other <u>jamro</u> kinds of animal-eating plants live in distant lands.   major

4. A <u>topli</u> will fly us there.   pilot

5. What is my <u>tomvie</u>?   motive

6. I'm just interested in watching a still, <u>lentsi</u> plant catch an insect.   silent

7. I hope that someday I'll see that <u>pruse</u> carnivorous plant, the Rajah pitcher plant.   super

8. I like <u>dacre</u> trees.   cedar

▶ **Write the Spelling Word that names each picture.**

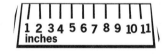

9. _____ ruler _____   11. _____ raven _____

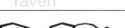

10. _____ paper _____   12. _____ spiders _____

Handwriting Tip: Do not make a loop when writing the letter *t*. Cross the *t* clearly, so that it doesn't look like an *l*. Write the Spelling Words below.

motive

13. pilot _____ pilot _____   14. native _____ native _____

SCHOOL-HOME CONNECTION With your child, look around your home or neighborhood and name things you see. Help your child list the VCV words.

Touch a Dream   **213**

Name _____

► **Write words from the box to complete the sentences.**

transformed	investigate	enthusiastically
decor	apparently	corridor

Dear Cousin,

You've got to see the **(1)** _____ decor _____ in our

classroom. A lot of my friends and I **(2)** _____ transformed _____

the room into a tropical rain forest! It looks so cool! You don't suspect

anything when you're outside in the **(3)** _____ corridor _____.

But when you walk into the room, wow! I've never written so

(4) _____ enthusiastically _____ about any class project before!

You should visit our school and **(5)** _____ investigate _____ for

yourself! The city newspaper is **(6)** _____ apparently _____

going to have a story about it. Watch for my picture!

Your cousin,

Aldo

► **Write the word from the box above that means the same as each word below.**

7. energetically _____ enthusiastically _____

8. research _____ investigate _____

9. seemingly _____ apparently _____

10. changed _____ transformed _____

TRY THIS! Think of a way you'd like to decorate your classroom or a room at home.
Write sentences that describe your decorations, using at least three
Vocabulary Words.

Harcourt

Name _____

Make inferences by putting together information from the text and your own knowledge and experience.

▶ **Read the ad. Then write *yes* or *no* to indicate whether a reader could correctly make that inference.**

Jungle Outfitters

We lead the safest, most exciting trips into the Amazon rain forest!

- Experienced guides.
- Paramedic or doctor accompanies each group.
- Travel by canoe and by foot deep into the rain forest.
- Price includes transportation and all meals for three weeks.
- Departures every six weeks.

Plan to bring cool, loose-fitting clothing, strong hiking boots, a canteen for drinking water, and a sleeping bag. You'll also need insect repellent and mosquito netting. Call today! 302-555-1000

1. It's hot in the rain forest. _____ yes

2. The trip will last about three weeks. _____ yes

3. People never get sick or hurt on the trip. _____ no

4. The travelers will be doing a lot of hiking. _____ yes

5. The travelers will sleep in hotels every night. _____ no

6. Mosquitoes could be a problem in the rain forest. _____ yes

7. There are no rivers in the rain forest. _____ no

8. Everybody loves to visit the rain forest. _____ no

9. Travelers in the rain forest are expected to find their own way around. _____ no

10. The travelers can probably leave heavy coats at home. _____ yes

Harcourt

SCHOOL-HOME CONNECTION With your child, read some newspaper advertisements. Then discuss what inferences can and cannot be made.

Name _____

▶ **Complete the story map below.** Possible responses are
given.

Main Characters	Setting
Aldo, Bolivia, Derek, Rory, DeDe, Mr. Peters, Lucette	the school's science room, now transformed into a rain forest

Problem

The sprinkler system is accidentally triggered, and no one can turn it off.

Important Events

Bolivia brings her parrot to the school's rain forest. Water begins falling hard from the ceiling after heat in the room triggers the sprinklers. After opening the windows, Mr. Peters sends Aldo to get the custodian. The assistant principal walks in and is scared by a snake in the room. Water is flowing out the door.

Solution

The custodian finally arrives and turns off the sprinklers.

▶ **How is the school's rain forest like a real one?**

Possible response: The school's rain forest has real rubber plants, a parrot,

two snakes, dirt, mud, and rain.

Name _____

▶ **Read each sentence. Then write your answer to each
statement about the underlined word.**

1. Kayla's uncle has several parrots that <u>he</u> trains for movies and
   television shows.

   He is _____ Kayla's uncle _____ .

2. Some parrots could already speak before her
   uncle got them, but he has taught <u>them</u> to
   say much more.

   Them refers to _____ parrots _____ .

3. Some of the birds talk a lot. <u>Others</u> can do funny tricks.

   Others means _____ other birds _____ .

4. Kayla laughed when she saw <u>one</u> lying on the floor of its cage and saying,
   "Sleepy bird!"

   One means _____ one bird or parrot _____ .

5. Several of the birds have been in movies. Kayla's favorite parrot, Joko, did

   <u>this</u>, too. *This* is what Joko has done. He has _____ been in movies _____ .

6. In <u>one</u>, he played the part of a wild parrot.

   One means _____ one movie _____ .

7. <u>He</u> even got to perch on a monkey's head!

   He is _____ Joko _____ .

8. Many parrots can learn to do tricks. Joko
   learned <u>some</u> very quickly.

   Some means _____ some tricks _____ .

9. A <u>few</u> are especially good actors.

   Few refers to a few _____ parrots _____ .

10. <u>They</u> seem to love the camera.

    They are _____ parrots _____ .

Name _____

The Down
and Up Fall

Extending
Vocabulary:
Connotation/
Denotation

▶ Write a word from the box that has a similar denotation
(dictionary or exact meaning) but a different connotation
(suggested meaning) than the underlined word
or words.

wolfing	stink	trampled	squeezed	deserted
show off	spattered	starving	peeked	sprinkle

1. First, Andy's dog <u>stepped on</u> my grandmother's flowers. _____trampled_____

2. The burning hot dogs created quite a <u>smell</u>. _____stink_____

3. By the time lunch was finally ready, we were all <u>hungry</u>. _____starving_____

4. We all laughed at Buzzy, who was <u>gulping</u> down his food. _____wolfing_____

5. My little cousin Alice started to <u>perform</u>. _____show off_____

6. John and I <u>looked</u> at a little bird's nest. _____peeked_____

7. We had just finished eating when it began to <u>rain</u>. _____sprinkle_____

8. All the leftover food was <u>covered</u> with rain. _____spattered_____

9. Everyone <u>got</u> under the picnic table. _____squeezed_____

10. By the time the rain stopped, the park was <u>empty</u>. _____deserted_____

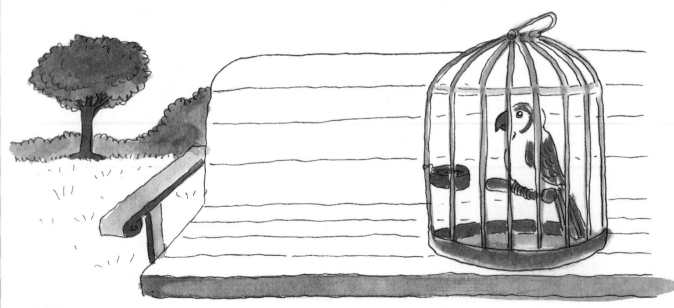

Harcourt

Name _____

▶ **Underline the prepositional phrase. Circle the preposition.**

1. Rubber plants grew (in) the rain forest.

2. Lucette perched (on) a high branch.

3. (After) a few minutes, she began talking.

4. She squawked (at) the people below.

5. A green snake (with) black markings appeared.

6. We almost fell (into) the pond.

7. We asked (for) a volunteer to lead us.

8. Our leader went ahead (of) us, and we
formed a line.

▶ **Complete each sentence with a prepositional phrase.** Responses will vary.

9. Bolivia brought her parrot _____.

10. _____, Lucette seemed content.

11. She preened her feathers _____.

12. She climbed _____ very carefully.

13. The students _____ clapped.

14. The green parrot then swooped _____.

15. _____ some students left.

16. Then Bolivia _____.

TRY THIS! Rewrite this sentence three times: *The students saw a parrot.*
Add a different prepositional phrase each time. How does the sentence's
meaning change?

Harcourt

Name _____

▶ **Find and circle the twelve misspelled words. Then write the words correctly on the lines.**

We've worked on (difrent) science projects. I can (rimember) each one.

(Begining) in the fall, we studied the solar system. Each planet had to spin in the right (derection). Getting all the planets going at the same time was (probly) the most (difficult) part of our project. The models took a lot of time and (enrgy) and our results were (excellant).

Everyone had to (descover) and share (importent) facts about life in the rain forest.

We're about to start working on (annother) science project. I can't (imagin) what it will be!

	SPELLING WORDS
	1. difficult
	2. probably
	3. beginning
	4. direction
	5. discover
	6. excellent
	7. important
	8. imagine
	9. energy
	10. remember
	11. different
	12. another

1. _different_   7. _energy_

2. _remember_   8. _excellent_

3. _Beginning_   9. _discover_

4. _direction_   10. _important_

5. _probably_   11. _another_

6. _difficult_   12. _imagine_

Handwriting Tip: Practice writing words you have problems with. Write the Spelling Words below.

$$important$$

13. difficult _difficult_   14. beginning _beginning_

SCHOOL-HOME CONNECTION With your child, write as many three syllable words that you can. Try to organize the words into groups, such as *ends with -tion (vacation)*.

Harcourt

Skills and Strategies Index

COMPREHENSION

Author's purpose
  and perspective 165–166, 172
Cause and effect 52–53, 60
Classify/Categorize 211
Compare and contrast 86, 91
Draw conclusions 78–79, 84
Fact and opinion 148–149, 157
Main idea and details 114–115, 120
Make generalizations 159, 187
Make inferences 197, 215
Make judgments 141
Predict outcomes 38–39, 44

Problem solving 122
Referents 217
Sequence 93–94, 98
Summarize and paraphrase 128–129, 134
Summarize the literature 2, 10, 16, 25, 31, 37, 45, 51, 61, 68, 77, 85, 92, 99, 106, 113, 121, 127, 135, 140, 147, 158, 164, 174, 180, 188, 196, 202, 210, 216
Vocabulary in context 189–190, 201
Words with more than one
meaning 175, 195

DECODING/PHONICS

Decoding long words 136, 173
Prefixes and suffixes 17–18, 24
Word identification strategies 26, 50

GRAMMAR

Abbreviations 103
Adjectives and articles 131
Adverbs 198
Clauses 65
Comparing with adjectives 137
Comparing with adverbs 206
Complete and simple predicates 41
Complete and simple subjects 34
Compound subjects and predicates 47
Contractions and negatives 192
Nouns
  Common and proper 81
  Possessive 95
  Singular and plural 88
Past and future tenses 177
Prepositional phrases 219

Prepositions 212
Present tense 169
Pronouns and antecedents 110
  Possessive pronouns 124
  Subject and object pronouns 117
Sentences 6
  Complex 73
  Declarative and interrogative 12
  Imperative and exclamatory 21
  Simple and compound 57
Subjects and predicates 28
Verbs 143
  Action and linking verbs 161
  Irregular verbs 183
  Main and helping verbs 153

LITERARY CONCEPTS

Characters' feelings and actions 11, 15
Elements of nonfiction
  (expository) 107–108
Figurative language 46

Narrative elements 3–4, 9
Point of view 32–33, 76
Theme 62–63

Skills and Strategies Index

SPELLING

Abbreviations 104
Adding -*ed* and -*ing* 178
Changing *y* to *i* 138
Contractions 193
Homophones 199
Possessive nouns 96
Prefixes *non-*, *in-*, and *re-* 132
Prefixes *un-* and *dis-* 125
"Silent" letters 184
Suffixes -*tion*, -*ness*, -*able*, -*less*, -*ful* 144
Unusual plurals 89
VCCV words 207
VCV words 213
Words that end with -*y* or -*ey* 118

Words with
/är/ 42
/âr/ 58
/əl/ 162
/ən/ 170
/ər/ 154
ie, *ei*, and *eigh* 111
long and short *a* 7
long and short *e* 13
long and short *i* 22
long and short *o* and *u* 29
/oi/ 82
/o͞o/ 35
/ôr/ 48
/ou/ 74
three syllables 220
/ûr/ 66

STUDY/RESEARCH SKILLS

Follow written directions 116
Graphic sources 203–205, 209
Library/Media center 19–20
Locating information 150–151, 156
Note taking 69–70
Outlining 71–72

Reference sources 167–168, 186
Search techniques 54–55
Skim and scan 181–182
Study strategies 100–101
Test taking 102, 146

VOCABULARY

Analogies 56
Antonyms 80, 130
Compound words 27
Connotation/Denotation 176, 218
Context clues 142
Figurative language/Similes 87
Homographs 160
Homophones 40

Multiple-meaning words 123
Regionalisms 191
Science words 109
Selection vocabulary 1, 8, 14, 23, 30, 36, 43, 49, 59, 67, 75, 83, 90, 97, 105, 112, 119, 126, 133, 139, 145, 155, 163, 171, 179, 185, 194, 200, 208, 214
Specialized words 152
Synonyms 5, 130
Word origins 64